ROCK AROUND THE CLOCK

THE RECORD THAT STARTED THE ROCK REVOLUTION!

BY JIM DAWSON

With a British Remembrance by Ian Whitcomb

Backbeat
Books
San Francisco

Published by Backbeat Books
600 Harrison Street, San Francisco, CA 94107
www.backbeatbooks.com
email: books@musicplayer.com

An imprint of CMP Information
Publishers of *Guitar Player*, *Bass Player*, *Keyboard*, and *EQ* magazines

Copyright © 2005 by Jim Dawson. All rights reserved. No part of this book covered by copyrights hereon may be reproduced or copied in any manner whatsoever without written permission, except in the case of brief quotations embodied in articles and reviews. For information, contact the publishers.

Distributed to the book trade in the US and Canada by
Publishers Group West, 1700 Fourth Street, Berkeley, CA 94710

Distributed to the music trade in the US and Canada by
Hal Leonard Publishing, P.O. Box 13819, Milwaukee, WI 53213

Cover Design by Richard Leeds — bigwigdesign.com
Composition by Michael Cutter

Library of Congress Cataloging-in-Publication Data

Dawson, Jim, 1944–
  Rock around the clock : the record that started the rock revolution! / by Jim Dawson.
     p. cm.
Includes bibliographical references (p. 191), discography (p. 185), and index.
ISBN 0-87930-829-X (alk. paper)
1. Haley, Bill. Rock around the clock. 2. Rock music—History and criticism. 3. Sound recordings—History. I. Title.
  ML3534.D378 2005
  782.42166—dc22
                    2005007381

Printed in the United States of America

05 06 07 08 09   5 4 3 2 1

CONTENTS

INTRODUCTION 5

CHAPTER 1: April Is the Coolest Month 7

CHAPTER 2: Rock Me With a Steady Roll! 11

CHAPTER 3: Let the Good Times Roll 20

CHAPTER 4: Yodelin' Bill Haley 26

CHAPTER 5: Calling All Comets 34

CHAPTER 6: Crazy Man, Crazy 50

CHAPTER 7: Put Your Glad Rags On 57

CHAPTER 8: Rockin' up in Seventh Heaven 71

CHAPTER 9: We'll Yell for More! 87

CHAPTER 10: Blackboard Jungle 113

CHAPTER 11: Rock Around the Clock Again 127

CHAPTER 12: Hollywood Rock 'n' Roll 144

CHAPTER 13: Hellbound Train to Waterloo 157
    (a British remembrance by former pop star Ian Whitcomb)

CHAPTER 14: When the Clock Strikes Twelve 170

CHAPTER 15: Rock Till Broad Daylight! 177

CHAPTER 16: For the Record 183

ACKNOWLEDGMENTS 189

BIBLIOGRAPHY 191

ABOUT THE AUTHOR 199

PHOTO CREDITS 201

INDEX 203

INTRODUCTION

"My throbbing heart shall rock thee day and night."
—William Shakespeare, Venus and Adonis (1593)

"Do, my Johnny Boker, come rock and roll me over, do, my Johnny Boker, do!"
—"Johnny Boker," a nineteenth-century American sea chantey

"Before Elvis, there was nothing," John Lennon said famously, but he should've known better. Before Elvis, there was Bill Haley and His Comets. Before Elvis, there was Haley's "Rock Around the Clock," the first rock 'n' roll record to go to No. 1 in America (July 1955) and, four months later, in the United Kingdom as well. Clocking in at a mere two minutes and eight seconds, "Rock Around the Clock" was the dividing point between pre-rock and rock, Hernando's Hideaway and Heartbreak Hotel, Tin Pan Alley and Sunset Strip, all that went before and all that came after. Its sales exceed twenty-five million copies, according to *Rolling Stone*. Other sources put the tally at three or four times that, since the song has appeared on countless anthologies. *The Guinness Book of Records* claims that only Bing Crosby's perennial "White Christmas" and Elton John's "Candle in the Wind" (the Princess Di edition) have sold more singles. In 2000 National Public Radio included "Rock Around the Clock" among "The 100 Most Important Musical Works of the 20th Century." *American Bandstand* host Dick Clark called it "the anthem of rock." To pioneer disc jockey Alan Freed it was "the daddy of rock and roll." At this moment, the record is playing or being downloaded somewhere in the world.

Bill Haley's "Rock Around the Clock" wasn't the first modern rock 'n' roll hit. It wasn't the first song about rocking around the clock. It wasn't the first song called "Rock Around the Clock." It wasn't even the first rendition of this particular song called "Rock Around the Clock." But it *was* the original rock 'n' roll giant, and on its strength Bill Haley and His Comets became the first international rock stars, as well as the only 1950s rock 'n' rollers to play on every continent (except the polar ones, where the lyric "rock around the clock tonight" could only truly apply).

By all rights, "Rock Around the Clock" should never have been a hit. It began as a patchwork of Jewish folk melody, minstrelsy, 1920s blues, and a TV theme song for late-night movies, and ended as an amalgam of nearly every popular American musical strain of the first half of the twentieth century. It was sung by a one-eyed, twenty-nine-year-old yodeling champ with a heavy jaw and a spit curl that couldn't hide his receding hairline. It was hastily recorded in less than a half hour and cobbled together from two unusable takes. It was released as the B-side of a song about a nuclear holocaust, and then forgotten after the record went nowhere. But thanks to a few unlikely twists and turns and bits of odd luck, "Rock Around the Clock" found its way to greatness, and Bill Haley was given a few good years to evangelize the globe in the service of rock 'n' roll. If Elvis Presley was the King, Bill Haley was John the Baptist.

"Rock Around the Clock" has appeared in over two dozen films and played over the opening credits of at least three of them, including the first rock 'n' roll movie. It has been the theme of a successful TV show. Over five hundred artists have recorded it in at least thirty languages. Among them are accordionist Myron Floren, Yiddish klezmer comedian Mickey Katz, the Deep River Boys gospel group, Mae West (produced by Ian Whitcomb), the Isley Brothers, Tiny Tim, the Sex Pistols, Chubby Checker, Henry Mancini & The Royal Philharmonic Pops Orchestra, Sha-Na-Na, Pat Boone, the Osmonds, Carl Perkins, Morton Fraser's Harmonica Gang (with the Hillbilly Polecats), and Chinese pop star Miss Yung Yung. John Lennon, he of the "Before Elvis" quote, produced a version of "Rock Around the Clock" by Harry Nilsson. There's even a "Rock Around the Clock" on paper by legendary "piano-roll perforator-musician" J. Lawrence Cook.

For several years now, the celebrity media have been making a big deal of announcing the arrival of the fiftieth anniversary of rock 'n' roll, pegging their commemorations on any number of early recordings and musical events, from Ike Turner's "Rocket 88" to Alan Freed's first sellout R&B concert to Elvis Presley's first Sun Records session, but the real beginning of rock 'n' roll as a phenomenon was July 2, 1955, when "Rock Around the Clock" climbed to the pinnacle of the American pop charts in the July 9 issue of *Billboard* magazine and heralded the arrival of the youth culture that eventually conquered the world. This is the story of that song and that record and the way they changed everything.

CHAPTER 1

APRIL IS THE COOLEST MONTH

Two girls in wide, colorful skirts danced a do-si-do in front of a double bass fiddle on the cover of the April 12, 1954, issue of *Life*, one of America's most cherished family magazines. A headline at their feet announced "Lively Fashions for Sub-Teens." Levitating above their carefree heads were the words: "Complete Story of H-Blast: Cities Study Disaster Plans." Inside this cozy weekly, near the front, black-and-white photos of a 1952 nuclear detonation in the Marshall Islands were laid out like frames in an army training film, displaying an ovum-shaped fireball, followed by a roiling mushroom of debris. "A sinister close-up shows the poisonous cloud surging up into the stratosphere, turgid with the remnants of Elugelab Island," said the caption. Far from this paroxysm, midway into the magazine, a Technicolor fashion spread called "Not Yet Thirteen" informed readers that because of a soaring birthrate during the early 1940s, "there are 4.2 million girls who have reached the ages of 10 to 12, enough to rate a new branch of the dress business devoted to their sizes and styles."

The parents of these children had retreated into tree-lined suburbs to raise them after the U.S. emerged from World War II nine years earlier as the only industrial nation still standing. Plenty of round-the-clock factory jobs and strong employee unions provided such a comfortable standard of living that for the first time in history most working people considered themselves prosperous enough to be middle-class—an enormous American bourgeoisie. The mass production of gypsum-board drywall allowed developers to throw up millions of tract homes the average family could afford, especially with the help of a generous G.I. Bill and low interest rates. Opulence replaced the destitution and rationing that had dogged the country for two decades, allowing Americans to lavish a disproportionate share of the world's wealth and resources on their princesses and princelings.

On that same April 12, a Monday, Bill Haley and His Comets drove to a New York City studio to record two songs. One of them was the story of a lucky guy and thirteen female companions who'd survived a hydrogen bomb explosion. It had been fashioned into a faintly humorous novelty, because in 1954 the American popular music industry didn't tolerate anything dark or subversive. The second number was "Rock Around the Clock," an uptempo twelve-bar dance ditty whose only seditious element was its siren call to an all-night party where folks could leave their proprieties at the door. Taken more figuratively, the song was an invocation for abandoning social responsibilities altogether, for the term "round the clock" in those days meant not just twenty-four hours, but—to use the twenty-first-century expression that replaced it—24/7.

And why not? Despite the nation's postwar prosperity, the last several years had been vaguely uneasy for everyone. A polio plague, transmitted like the common cold, had been stalking the land and taking its heaviest toll on children and young adults, leaving them paralyzed or gasping for a last breath. In 1952, the worst year of the epidemic, polio claimed nearly 58,000 victims. There would be no sign of a cure until April 12, 1955, exactly a year after the Comets recorded "Rock Around the Clock," when Dr. Jonas Salk publicly announced the discovery of a vaccine.

Elsewhere, the Atomic Age and a Cold War with the Soviet Union had dangled an apocalyptic sword over America's split-level Eden. Only a month earlier, on March 1, the Atomic Energy Commission had detonated its most powerful H-bomb yet—capable of incinerating ten New York Cities—on a South Pacific atoll named Kwajalein, then hastily tried to cover up the fact that the eighteen-mile-high mushroom cloud had contaminated everything within a hundred miles, including several inhabited villages. That same commission, on that very April 12, convened the first of a series of hearings to determine whether Dr. Robert Oppenheimer, the father of the atomic bomb, had been slipping vital information to foreign governments. The Congressional House Committee on Un-American Activities, led by Senator Joe McCarthy, was pursuing Communist spies in Washington and getting ready in nationally televised hearings, slated to begin later in the month, to take on Red sympathizers in the U.S Army. National paranoia had burrowed so deep that even levelheaded farmers and airplane pilots were sighting flying saucers from Mars. Whether folks knew it or not, they needed emotional release from all this gloom, and many were ready to dance to the break of day, for it might be a thermonuclear dawn, the last they'd ever see, or would want to.

As Bill Haley already knew, Americans had a remedy for their malaise right in their own back yard—or at least on the other side of the railroad tracks. It was called rhythm and blues, a mix of blues and jazz and boogie-woogie that coalesced in the mid-1940s when Negro big bands were forced by wartime rationing and the predations of draft boards to trim down into smaller, more swinging combos. Most R&B artists had turned their backs on the meticulous craft of the Great American Songbook, opting instead for the emotional vernacular of the blues. In fact, R&B music inspired the two songs Haley and his musicians recorded that April day. Yet the people who had developed it still lived in a parallel universe whose separation was mandated by law. The U.S. Supreme Court was still five weeks away from its May 17th *Brown v. Board of Education of Topeka* decision ending compulsory racial segregation in the nation's public schools, and Rosa Parks wouldn't sit down in the front seat of a Montgomery, Alabama, bus for another twenty months.

So America was sleepwalking through the doldrums. The No. 1 song that day was a comforting Tin Pan Alley confection called "Wanted" by Perry Como, a silky crooner from the big band era. Even the biggest hit on the rhythm and blues charts was a 1940s Rodgers & Hammerstein pop-gospel restorative from the Broadway musical *Carousel* called "You'll Never Walk Alone," done up in resonant grandeur by baritone Roy Hamilton. *TV Guide* predicted big things ahead for that week's cover boy, a wavy-haired balladeer on *The Milton Berle Show* named Charlie Applewhite, whom the magazine dubbed "Berle's Gift to the Bobbysoxers." (Decca would release Applewhite's "No One but You" and the Comets' "Rock Around the Clock" back to back, with consecutive catalog numbers.)

Few suspected that a raucous, mood-altering musical revolution was in the works. Though Hank Ballard's "Work With Me, Annie" had come out a week earlier and Big Joe Turner's "Shake, Rattle, and Roll" arrived that very day, what we now recognize as rock 'n' roll was still nascent. Disc jockey Alan Freed was spinning R&B records in Cleveland. Chuck Berry was a part-time St. Louis hairdresser whose big break wouldn't come for another thirteen months. Bo

Diddley was working as an auto mechanic in Southside Chicago. Elvis Presley was driving a truck for Crown Electric in Memphis. Buddy Holly was a high school junior in Lubbock, Texas, and in a small Minnesota tank town Eddie Cochran was getting ready to graduate. So was Don Everly, two years ahead of his sophomore brother, Phil, in Knoxville, Tennessee. Johnny Cash was stationed with the U.S. Air Force in West Germany and Gene Vincent was a U.S. Navy boilerman based in Norfolk, Virginia. Carl Perkins was gigging in honky-tonks around Jackson, Mississippi, on a $3 guitar for $2 a night—plus all the moonshine he could drink. In Faraday, Louisiana, Jerry Lee Lewis was a high school dropout with delusions of singing Hank Williams songs on the popular *Louisiana Hayride* radio show. Ricky Nelson, almost fourteen years old, was part of the perfect Eisenhower American family on a Hollywood TV sitcom. Sam Cooke was a nineteen-year-old tenor in a crisp white suit, touring with a gospel group called the Soul Stirrers. A few miles north of where Bill Haley was recording, Frankie Lymon (in Harlem) was eleven years old and Dion DiMucci (in the Bronx) was fifteen. Little Richard Penniman had already recorded as a blues artist, but nothing had happened and now he was back home with his mother in Macon, Georgia, washing dishes at the local Greyhound bus terminal coffee shop. Though Ray Charles was a successful blues entertainer with hits on the R&B charts, he was still seven months away from recording the electrifying "I've Got a Woman" that supercharged his career. Fats Domino had recorded a couple of modest pop hits in the early fifties, but his breakthrough single, "Ain't That a Shame," was still a year ahead of him.

As far as rock 'n' roll was concerned, Bill Haley and His Comets were the only game in town on April 12, 1954, when they slipped quietly into the studio and laid down "Rock Around the Clock."

CHAPTER 2

ROCK ME WITH A STEADY ROLL!

Blues is a sixteenth-century English word that has variously meant sorrow, depression, ennui, and despair. That may explain why it didn't become a common member of the optimistic American vernacular until around 1910, when piano roll companies began selling ragtime songs with *blues* in the title for that middle-class parlor amenity, the player piano. The first man to popularize the blues was a black Memphis song publisher named William C. Handy, who repackaged old Negro folk songs and field hollers as public entertainment by straightening up their rambling bar structures, eliminating the sad notes, and sanitizing the lyrics; in other words, he bleached out the authentic blues elements, then called his songs the blues. In 1914 the sheet music for Handy's "Memphis Blues" became a brisk seller, followed two years later by "St. Louis Blues" and, as a tribute to Memphis' black main thoroughfare, "Beale Street Blues." The Columbia Phonograph Company's white studio orchestra turned all three into popular recordings.

Then in 1917 came the first jazz recording, the Original Dixieland "Jass" Band's whinnying and kicking "Livery Stable Blues," a surprise hit that changed the musical landscape just in time for the waning days of the First World War and the cultural upheaval that followed. This band also introduced, thanks to the limitations of early recording technology, another important element to twentieth-century music. The Victor Record Machine Company had begun to standardize the speed of commercial records at 78 revolutions per minute with its 1901 Victrola, but the ten-inch shellac "78" couldn't comfortably contain much more than three minutes of music. A recording supervisor often had to abridge a piece of music to make it fit. But the Original Dixieland "Jass" Band devised another way of shoehorning its performances onto one side of a record: They sped up their songs, until some of their early recordings, such as the 1917 hit "Indiana," sounded like runaway trains. As buyers responded enthusiastically to these quicker tempos, musicians cranked up their live performances. Before long, jazz bands were playing at full tilt, faster than music had ever been played before.

Meanwhile, it seemed that everybody was writing blues songs. For example, in 1919 two Jewish tunesmiths sitting in a cramped office in a Philadelphia downtown building wrote "I've Got the Cryin' Blues," with the lyric "Just like a baby I'm cryin', cryin' 'cause I feel so sad, I got the cryin' blues." The lyricist was a skinny youngster named Max C. Freedman, practicing up for "Rock Around the Clock," a song he would patch together three decades later. But like the other blues songs of its time, "I've Got the Cryin' Blues" was a Tin Pan Alley ragtime concoction. The word blues was simply a hot commercial tag for marketing songs, just as rock 'n' roll would be in the 1950s.

In the summer of 1920 a dapper, light-skinned New York composer named Perry Bradford convinced Fred Hager at the struggling Okeh Phonograph Company to cut a song he'd written called "Harlem Blues." The only person who could do it justice, he told Hager, was Mamie Smith, a stocky, thirty-year-old black vaudevillian whom Columbia—Okeh's parent company—had signed earlier in the year. Smith had already recorded two of Bradford's songs, but they were old-fashioned ballads that any white entertainer like Sophie Tucker or Nora Bayes could have handled. "Harlem Blues" was different. Bradford had tailored it especially for Miss Smith and her all-black band, the Jazz Hounds. He knew that during the past several years, far beyond the skyline of the traditional music business and tempered by grueling days and nights in the crucibles of carnival tents, tobacco barns, and shabby black theaters around the country, women like Mamie Smith and their male jazz accompanists had been crafting a new, more exciting style of blues. In their interplay the musicians had learned to vocalize with their instruments, and the singers had developed extravagant ways of mimicking the pyrotechnics of the cornetists and trombonists, as well as the rhythms of the pianists and banjo players. Already there were more than a dozen blues queens touring on the "chit'lin circuit" of black venues across the South and Midwest, drawing crowds wherever they appeared. But the only one under contract to a record company was Mamie Smith.

Fred Hager agreed to record Bradford's song on one condition. The title had to go. "Harlem Blues" was too "colored" for what the company perceived to be its buying public. So when Mamie Smith and her five Jazz Hounds went into a studio on August 10, 1920, she sang a slightly altered number called "Crazy Blues," the first real blues recording. Within four months the song was so popular that Columbia's pressing facilities struggled to keep up with the demand. Its success revealed that blacks, particularly those who'd come north for jobs during the previous decade, could afford to buy records, and whites were willing to cross the color line if the music was interesting. Suddenly every major record company scrambled to sign its own authentic female blues belter—and W. C. Handy's former music publishing partner, Harry H. Pace, decided the time was right for America's first black-owned record company.

Like Perry Bradford, Pace had been frustrated by record executives refusing to place his songs with black artists. Even with dialect material like "I's Gwine Back to Dixie" (a 1917 hit for soprano Alma Gluck), companies carried on the blackface minstrel tradition by using whites. In the rare instances when popular Negro entertainers got the chance to record, they were given pop songs and directed to use white elocution. "[P]honograph companies were not recording the voices of Negro singers and musicians [and] would not entertain my thought of recording a colored musician or colored voice," Pace wrote to author and essayist Roi Ottley in 1939. "I therefore determined to form my own company and make such recordings as I believed would sell."

Harry Pace named his label Black Swan Records in honor of Elizabeth Taylor Greenfield, a former slave whose music recitals around the world had made her famous in the nineteenth century as "the Black Swan." The company slogan touted every Black Swan release as being "The Only Genuine Colored Record—Others Are Only Passing for Colored." With a $30,000 grubstake he opened his office in the basement of his home in Harlem, found a professional studio downtown that would record his black artists as long as they didn't show up during regular business hours, and located a pressing plant a thousand miles away, in Wisconsin, willing to manufacture a black businessman's platters. His first hit, Ethel Waters's "Down Home Blues," sold half a million records in six months.

With Black Swan up and running, Pace found a twenty-seven-year-old vaudevillian named Trixie Smith. More handsome than pretty, Smith was a light-skinned Atlanta girl who had gone to college and then journeyed to New York City to find her fortune in show business. Though her voice was thin, she could sing everything from light classics to blues and minstrelsy with gusto. The *Chicago Defender*, one of the country's major black newspapers, later called her "a pleasing singer of humorous Negro songs to which she imparted a trick of delivery that kept her in demand by the managers." Her first record, "Trixie's Blues," sold well enough to assure her a couple of years of steady work.

For her fourth recording session, on a September evening in 1922, Smith went into a studio with pianist Fletcher Henderson and his Jazz Masters to cut two songs. One was written, or perhaps adapted from a black street song, by J. Berni Barbour. Not much is known about Barbour except that in 1903, in Manhattan, he co-founded America's first black music publishing company. Like any ambitious songwriter, Barbour catered to whatever the public was buying. He'd already written a couple of moderately popular ragtime songs. For Trixie Smith's recording session, however, he introduced an unusual blues that most white record labels wouldn't have touched. It bore the eyebrow-arching title of "My Man Rocks Me (With One Steady Roll)."

In a sharp, girlish contralto, Smith projected herself into the low-fidelity recording machine's cornucopia mouthpiece as if she were reaching for the last balcony seats of a ramshackle theater. In the opening verse she explained that "I feel so happy, I have a smile...since my baby came back home to stay, night and day." She asked the listener to "don't let it out" to any other woman about her "daddy," because—and here we go into the chorus: "My man rocks me with a steady roll, there's no slippin' when he once takes hold." There it was, *rock* and *roll* in the same line, in 1922. But it was the next lyric that people would remember most about the song: "I looked at the clock and the clock struck one, I said, 'Now, daddy, ain't we got fun,' oh he was rockin' me with one steady roll." In the next chorus Trixie "looked at the clock and the clock struck six, I said, 'Daddy, you know I like that fix,'" and so on, until she looked at the clock and the clock struck ten, "I said, 'Glory, *aaaay*-men!'" Though the song was obviously a sexual celebration about how good and for how long she was getting it—and the onomatopoeic repetition of the word *clock* made it clear what she was getting—Trixie sounded playful, even gleeful, but never salacious.

Still, the general public may not have been ready for "My Man Rocks Me (With One Steady Roll)" when Black Swan released it in January 1923, or perhaps the company was already having the promotional and financial problems that would sink it by the end of the year. The record sold well in several cities, especially Chicago, where it was a big favorite with black audiences,

Trixie Smith's 1923 blues, "My Man Rocks Me (With One Steady Roll)," brought the words "rock" and "roll" together on record for the first time.

but the song was destined never to be a major commercial hit. And yet something in it convinced other recording artists on major labels to try their luck, including the Southern Quartet (1924), the Golden Gate Orchestra (1924), Harold Ortli's Ohio State Collegians (a white jazz group on Okeh Records, 1925), Charles Creath's Jazz-O-Maniacs (1925), Husk O'Hare's Footwarmers (a white group on Vocalion, 1928), Jimmie Noone's Apex Club Orchestra, with vocalist May Alix (1929), and blues guitarist Tampa Red's Hokum Jazz Band (1929), featuring Frankie "Half-Pint" Jaxon, a Harlem female impersonator who moaned and squealed like a woman in the throes of something more than religious ecstasy.

From the very first remakes, the word *daddy*—blues slang for a gentleman sexually or financially capable of keeping a woman happy—replaced *man*, prompting a title change to "My Daddy Rocks Me," with the parenthesized "With a Steady Roll" usually omitted. More important, these artists dropped Barbour's opening verse and went straight to the catchy chorus, "My daddy rocks me with one steady roll...."

Writer Studs Terkel recalled hearing a raw variation of the song at Chicago's Dreamland ballroom in 1924, more than a year after Trixie Smith's recording. "Always, toward the end of the night," Terkel wrote, "comes the slow blues for which everybody is waiting.

> My daddy rocks me in a steady jelly roll
> My daddy rocks me and he never lets go
> I look at the clock and the clock strikes eight
> Oh, daddy, take it out before it gets too late...."

The song became influential enough in the ongoing story of the blues that it spurred answer records like the Bucktown Five's "Steady Rollin' Blues" (1924), Lil Johnson's "Rock That Thing" (1929), Ikey Robinson's "Rock Me Mama" (1929), and Hot Shot Willie's "Rollin' Mama Blues" (1932). Delta bluesman Robert Johnson responded a few years later with "I'm a Steady Rollin' Man" (1937), the same year that Georgia White sang "Rock Me, Daddy." The clamor became so great that Decca Records eventually lured semi-retired Trixie Smith back into a New York studio in 1938 to record a two-part remake of her old song with jazz clarinetist Sidney Bechet.

Cleveland-based bandleader Harold Ortli's herky-jerky, speeded-up 1924 recording, aimed at young Jazz Age dancers, was primarily an instrumental with only an eight-bar vocal interlude, but singer Clarence Buck used his moment in the limelight to transform the whole point of the song when he sang: "Daddy rocks me with a steady roll, naw there ain't no steppin' when he takes hold...." It wasn't unusual in those days for a male vocalist to present a song from a woman's point of view, or vice versa. A recording was a performance, like a play, and the singer took on the role as written by the composer, so there was nothing overtly homoerotic in Clarence Buck rockin' with Daddy. The real significance was that he supplanted "steppin'" for "slippin'"—moving the song out of the bedroom and into the ballroom, where Daddy was moving slow and easy, pulling his partner close and undulating his midsection against hers instead of doing the latest dance step. Going from grinding in bed to grinding on the dance floor suggested that as early as the mid-1920s in some quarters—in Cleveland, anyway, where a shrine to rock 'n' roll music would be built sixty years later—rock and roll meant dirty dancing.

Rock and roll became *Billboard*-chart ready as soon as two Hollywood film studio songwriters, Richard Whiting ("Hooray for Hollywood") and Sidney Clare ("Ma! He's Makin' Eyes at Me"), clicked together in 1934 with "On the Good Ship Lollipop" for child actress Shirley Temple in the movie *Bright Eyes*. Another song Whiting and Clare had written for the six-year-old star was an innocent, light-footed number called "Rock and Roll," but possibly because of the title's sexual tinge, Fox Pictures wouldn't let the curly-headed moppet anywhere near it. So the tunesmiths passed "Rock and Roll" along to the Boswell Sisters, three hip white chicks from New Orleans known for their breezy rhythms and tight, roller-coaster harmonies. The Boswells recorded the song for the Brunswick label and performed it in a low-budget Jack Benny film called *Transatlantic Merry-Go-Round*. "There's romance while we dance, it's the rollin' rockin' rhythm of the sea," the sexy siblings chanted as they rowed onstage in a rocking rowboat, while cardboard waves rolled by. "Rock and roll like a rockin' chair...rock and roll, rollin' rockaway...rock and roll, rollin' rockalong...." Their "Rock and Roll" became a Top 10 hit in November 1934.

Three years later Ella Fitzgerald, shimmering in white silk in front of Chick Webb's swing orchestra, recorded a slow blues called "Rock It for Me," in which her reference to rock and roll's terpsichorean properties seemed so casual as to be well understood by whomever was listening: "Now it's true that once upon a time the opera was the thing, but today the rage is rhythm and rhyme, so won't you satisfy my soul with the rock and roll, you can't be tame while the band is playing, it ain't no shame to keep your body swaying, they beat it out in the minor key. Oh, rock it for me." Clearly rock and roll meant expressive dancing—in this case slowly, but with all body parts in sensual motion. Released as a Chick Webb single on Decca Records, "Rock It for Me" charted for one week in February 1938 and inspired several other artists, including white jazz singer Mildred Bailey and black bandleader Jimmie Lunceford, to record bouncier, more syncopated versions.

That same year, another black bandleader, Erskine Hawkins, made his recording debut with an instrumental called "Rockin' Rollers Jubilee." Like Lunceford's jived-up version of "Rock It for Me," it was a swing number meant to get the dancers on the floor. And the dance they were doing in 1938— whether they were young blacks or, increasingly, white hipsters—was the

Released on the Brunswick and Columbia labels, the Boswell Sisters' "Rock and Roll" was a 1934 hit from the film Transatlantic Merry-Go-Round.

lindy hop, better known as the jitterbug, essentially the same steps and body movements teenagers would be doing (though much less acrobatically) to a rock 'n' roll beat on *American Bandstand* twenty years later. In other words, for a short time in the late thirties, to rock and roll was to jitterbug to a swing rhythm. Why the term never crossed over into white parlance at the time is anybody's guess.

In the 1940s, during the war, black big bands slimmed down into six- and seven-man combos playing a mix of swing, boogie-woogie, and blues. Some called this music "jump blues," but the official designation codified by *Billboard* late in the decade was "rhythm and blues." One of its early stars was a handsome, gravelly-voiced shouter from Nebraska named Wynonie Harris. By 1944, just a year after the death of Trixie Smith, Harris appropriated the clock-watching gimmick from "My Man Rocks Me" for his own risqué blues number, "Round the Clock," which he performed in black nightclubs throughout the country, improvising new verses for as long—and making them as dirty—as the audience would allow.

When Harris was asked to record his first solo session in 1945, he cleaned up "Round the Clock" and played the good-rockin' daddy with a steady roll to the hilt: "Well, I looked at the clock, the clock struck one, she said, 'Come on, Daddy, let's have a little more fun,' yes, we was rollin', yes, we rolled a long time.... We looked at the clock, the clock struck two, I said, 'Tell me, pretty mama, is your daddy thrillin' you?'" And so on, as Teddy Edwards's languid tenor saxophone moaned and sighed in the background.

"Round the Clock" didn't chart, but it remained one of Harris's enduring numbers. At least half a dozen other blues performers recorded it over the next two years, including Big Joe Turner (as "Round the Clock Blues"), Willie Bryant ("Blues Around the Clock"), and former Count Basie vocalist Jimmy Rushing ("Jimmy's Round the Clock Blues"). All were basically the same song, but each record credited a different composer—and neither Trixie Smith nor J. Berni Barbour was among them. By now, looking up at the clock in the throes of coitus was a standard blues idiom, there for the taking.

As fate would have it, Harris was responsible for bringing rocking back into the black mainstream in 1948 with a song called "Good Rockin' Tonight," one of the year's biggest sellers on the R&B charts and an inspiration for Elvis Presley six years later. From then on, rockin' and rollin' was a staple of rhythm and blues, including four recordings of four different songs titled "Rock and Roll" between 1948 and 1950 alone.*

They set the stage for a little-known 1950 recording by an obscure black comedian backed by the tenor saxophonist who had frantically honked behind Wynonie Harris on "Good Rockin' Tonight." The song was called "Rock Around the Clock," and it sank without a trace, without anybody ever hearing it. Or so it seemed at the time.

---

*"Rock and Roll" by Paul Bascomb (1948), "Rock and Roll" by Wild Bill Moore (1949), "Rock and Roll" by Doles Dickens (1949), and "Rock and Roll" by John Lee Hooker (1950). There was also "Rock and Roll Blues" by Erline Harris (1949).

CHAPTER 3

LET THE GOOD TIMES ROLL

In the 1970s Sam Theard was an elderly, horse-faced character actor enjoying a recurring role in the last seasons of the NBC sitcom *Sanford and Son* and showing up in small parts in black film comedies, including Richard Pryor's *Which Way Is Up?* Yet when he died in Los Angeles on December 7, 1982, at age seventy-eight, his passing went unnoticed outside of one or two esoteric blues magazines. Chances are good you've never heard of him. But if you glance over his twenty-one-year recording and songwriting career—from his first session in 1929 to his last known recording date in 1950—Theard's effect on R&B and rock 'n' roll is considerable.

Sam Theard was born in New Orleans on October 10, 1904, but not much is known about his early years beyond his claim to have joined the circus after leaving high school. By the end of the 1920s, when guitarist Tampa Red introduced him to a black record producer named J. Mayo Williams in Chicago, Theard was already a popular tent show singer and chit'lin comic known as Lovin' Sam From Down in 'Bam, based on a traditional minstrel figure popularized by the Peerless Quartet's 1917 hit, "Musical Sam From Alabam." During the next ten years Theard waxed over fifty songs. A couple of them were straight blues, but with his sandpaper voice and his knack for writing or appropriating "hokum" songs loaded with double entendres and gritty details about Negro life, he mostly recorded novelties like "She's Givin' It Away" and "I'm Crazy 'Bout My Bozo"—all delivered in the insinuating Southern idiom of minstrel shows.

One of the earliest songs Theard put together for Brunswick Records was "You Rascal, You," a betrayed husband's bitter lamentation that began with the line "I'll be glad when you're dead, you rascal, you." Nothing much happened to his 1929 record, but two years later one of his Brunswick labelmates, white cornetist Red Nichols, recorded a tidied-up version that, among other things, omitted Theard's original threat to castrate the man who wouldn't "leave my wife alone." Its modest sales in the pop market prompted yet another Brunswick artist, Harlem bandleader Cab Calloway, to try his luck with "You Rascal, You" for the jazz market. When Louis Armstrong covered it for Okeh Records with an over-the-top vocal performance, the Fleischer Brothers, a couple of Hollywood animators, showcased him mau-mauing the song with bug-eyed magnificence in a surreal Betty Boop cartoon. Both the Calloway and Armstrong renditions sold well enough in late 1931 to list in *Billboard*'s sales charts. Then, in a grace note early the following year, Brunswick handed the song to its hot new black singing quartet, the Mills Brothers, who were able to smooth out enough of the rough surfaces of "You Rascal, You" to turn it into a national pop sensation and put a little cash in Sam Theard's pocket.

In the 1930s he recorded under several names, including Spo Dee O Dee, an appellation he also fashioned into a novelty song called "Spo-De-O-Dee" that he laid down in 1937 for Vocalion Records and again in 1940 for Decca. Under various spellings, "spo-de-o-dee"—taken from the word "spode," slang for semen probably inspired by the china white color of Josiah Spode porcelain—was one of Theard's many euphemisms for sexual intercourse: "Adam met Eve in the Garden of Eden, that's where it first begun; Adam said to Eve, 'Let's spo-de-o-dee, come on, let's have some fun.'" A decade later, his producer, J. Mayo Williams, borrowed the term; working with another blues singer named Stick McGhee, he needed four nonsense syllables to replace a lyric in one of McGhee's bawdy numbers called "Drinkin' Wine, Motherfucker." The new "Drinkin' Wine, Spo-Dee-O-Dee" became one of the biggest R&B hits of 1949.

Theard was one of the first artists signed to Decca Records, later the home of Bill Haley, and in 1936 he made a recording that in many ways was a precursor to the jived-up hokum that the popular black artist Louis Jordan became known for a few years later. It was called "New Rubbing on That Darned Old Thing," an elaboration of a song he'd recorded earlier (and which the Grateful Dead would reprise over thirty years later as "The Rub"). Featuring a rocking five-man back-up band called Oscar's Chicago Swingers, "New Rubbing on That Darned Old Thing" came as close to being forties rhythm and blues as anything recorded in the thirties. Like most of Theard's songs, it was a setup for lewd wordplay. His girlfriend had let him use her washboard: "She said, 'Papa, don't ya rub so rough, when you hear me holler then that's enough.'" One lyric that catches the ear is "I kept rubbin', the clock struck six, she said, 'You got time to get your kicks.'" Since Theard was working off and on with Tampa Red's Hokum Boys at about the time they recorded "My Daddy Rocks Me (With One Steady Roll)" in 1929, he was certainly aware of the earlier song.

In the 1940s he "collaborated" with Louis Jordan on a couple of songs—which means, in fact, that Jordan, like many bandleaders, cut himself in on half of Theard's composer credits (and royalties) as his payment for recording them. Theard's "You Can't Get That No More," an update of an earlier song he'd written for Tampa Red, became one of Jordan's biggest pop hits in 1944, but it was "Let the Good Times Roll" (credited on Jordan's original record to writers Spo-de-o-de and Jordan's wife, Fleecie Moore) that assures Theard's place in blues history. As Jordan himself would later admit to writer Arnold Shaw, "'Let the Good Times Roll' was by Sam Theard, a comedian." "Let the Good Times

Sam Theard, pictured here in the late 1960s, wrote several seminal R&B songs, including Louis Jordan's blues anthem, "Let the Good Times Roll."

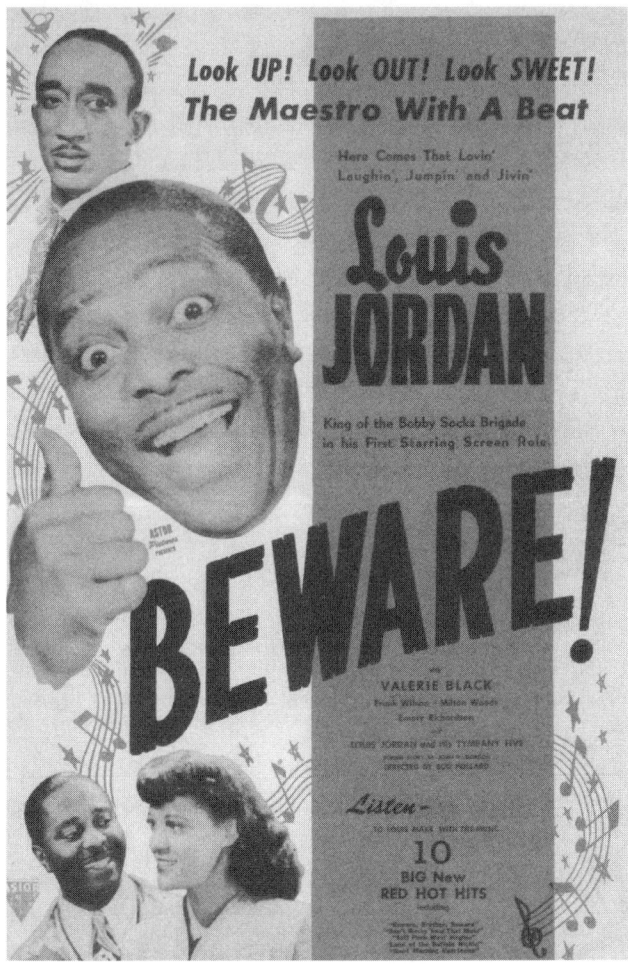

Bandleader, saxophonist, vocalist, and occasional film comedian Louis Jordan was America's top-selling black recording artist in the 1940s.

Roll"—with lyrics like "Hey, everybody, Mr. Jordan's in town, I got a dollar and a quarter and I'm just rarin' to clown; but don't let nobody play me cheap, I got fifty cents more than I'm gonna keep"—is now a blues anthem that has been recorded by B.B. King, Ray Charles, Muddy Waters, Eric Clapton, Herbie Hancock, Quincy Jones, and countless others. It was the showpiece song that King, Willie Dixon, Etta James, Big Jay McNeely, and several other R&B legends performed on the 1987 Grammy Awards. *Let the Good Times Roll* was also the title of a 1972 concert film recorded at Madison Square Garden, starring Bill

Haley and His Comets. (Shirley & Lee's likewise enduring 1956 pop hit, "Let the Good Times Roll," is a different song entirely.)

And now, to give Sam Theard his share of rock 'n' roll glory, let's move ahead to 1950, when as Spo-Dee-Odee he teamed up with tenor saxophonist Hal Singer, whose overheated instrumental blow-out, "Cornbread," had been a No. 1 R&B hit in 1947. Singer had also provided energetic accompaniment on Wynonie Harris' "Good Rockin' Tonight" in 1948. Now, two years later, he and Theard got together to record a song for Mercury Records called "Rock Around the Clock." Though both men shared writing credit, Theard likely penned the song and Singer cut himself in because the session (and the record) was under his name. Their "Rock Around the Clock" was a shuffle that began with a few bars of riffing trumpets and saxophones taken straight off half a dozen Louis Jordan records. Then Sam Theard's gruff voice barked, "Let's rock," answered by a chorus of band members: "We're gonna rock, rock around the clock." After a few more bars of call-and-response, Theard broke into the verse: "One for the money, two for the show, three make ready, four let's go, let's rock...."

Band: "We're gonna rock, rock around the clock...."

In the final verse, Theard sang, "Come on now, let's carry on, we're gonna rock till the break of dawn, let's rock...."

The overall construction of this "Rock Around the Clock" is different from the later hit record, but the repeated line of "rock around the clock" is similar in melody to what a group called Sonny Dae & His Knights would sing three years later when they introduced the first recording of the now-famous "Rock Around the Clock," except the Knights accented the words differently than Theard and added "tonight" at the end of the line.

Theard: "We're gonna *rock* [pause] *rock* around the clock...."

The Knights: "We're gonna *rock* a-*round* the *clock* tonight...."

Was Max C. Freedman listening to this 1950 "Rock Around the Clock" when he wrote his biggest hit? We'll most likely never know. Though Mercury was a major label, it had picked up Theard's version in some kind of lease deal and put it out because Hal Singer was still popular. *Billboard*'s reviewer was unimpressed: "Formula good-rocker gets lost before it gets started, as ensemble chanting and instrumental work are muddled." In short, it wasn't a very good recording, and sales were negligible. But one thing is certain: Theard's "Rock Around the Clock" fit naturally into his body of work, whereas the later "Rock Around the Clock" was unlike anything Freedman had ever written.

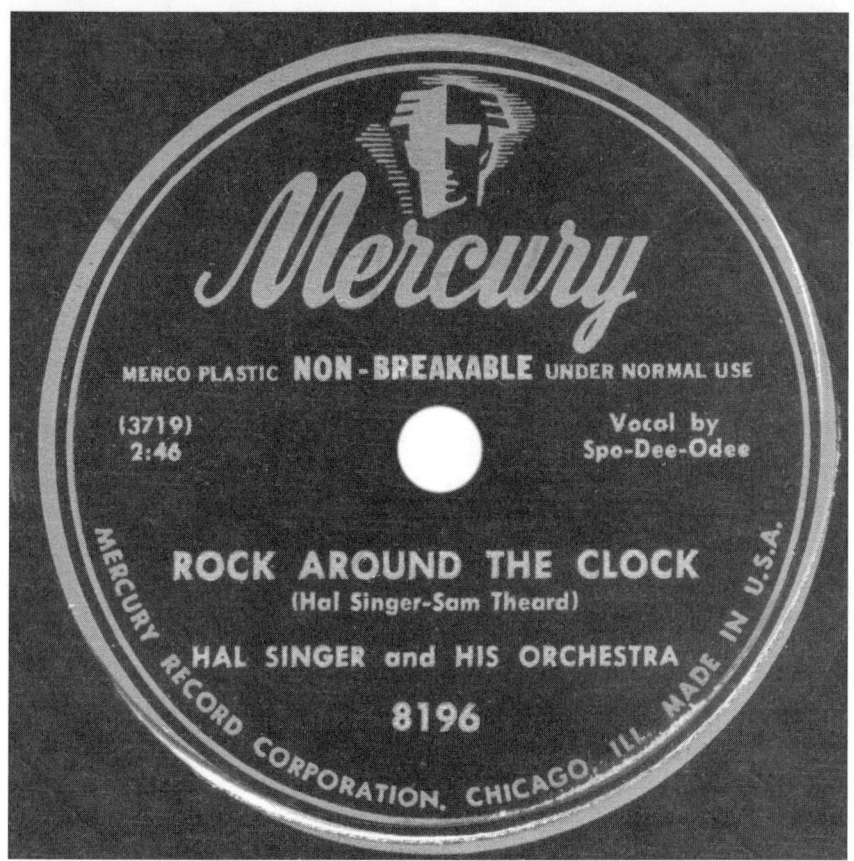

Elements of Sam "Spo-Dee-Odee" Theard's 1950 "Rock Around the Clock" showed up three years later in Max C. Freedman's more famous song.

In 1952, Wally Mercer, a black, forty-year-old boogie-woogie pianist from Florida, recorded "Rock Around the Clock" for Dot Records. It was a remarkably modern-sounding rock 'n' roll performance that got a lot of airplay in Atlanta, Georgia—and seemingly nowhere else. The song bore absolutely no resemblance in melody, lyric, or structure to Sam Theard's "Rock Around the Clock," nor to the other "Rock Around the Clock" that Max C. Freedman would write the following year.

But something was definitely in the air.

CHAPTER 4

YODELIN' BILL HALEY

William John Clifton Haley Jr., the man destined to bring "Rock Around the Clock" to life, was born July 6, 1925, in Highland Park, Michigan, a working-class suburb of Detroit. His part-Cherokee father, a shy high school dropout with a speech impediment, had come from rural Kentucky to work as a mechanic in a gas station. At age thirty he married a much younger girl, Maude Green, who had emigrated from England with her family just before World War I. They shared more than a fair degree of musicality. Bill Sr. was a good banjo and mandolin picker, and Maude, a religious woman, played organ at church and taught classical piano to local youngsters.

When their son Billy was four years old, a Detroit doctor performing an operation to repair an inner ear ailment accidentally severed an optic nerve. Nobody realized what had happened until one day Bill Sr. noticed that as the boy was looking up into the sunny sky, he used his hand to shade only the right side of his face. The left eye was dead.

A couple of years later, as the Depression began to wreck Detroit's industrial economy, Bill Sr. packed up the family and relocated to Boothwyn, Pennsylvania, where Maude's family lived. As soon as he got a job at a local Viscose plant, he moved to nearby Chester, an ugly Delaware River factory town fifteen miles southwest of Philadelphia that was swathed in a perpetual stink from its giant Scott Paper mill. Chester's most famous native at that time was Ethel Waters, America's top black recording star in the twenties and early thirties, whose first hit on Black Swan Records had paved the way for Trixie

Smith's "My Man Rocks Me." It was also the birthplace of Jimmy Preston, a black musician twelve years older than Billy Jr. who would later provide him with his first hit song.

After a year of living in a downtown tenement, the Haleys moved to a one-story house a few miles outside of town in the unincorporated farming village of Booth's Corner. There, hampered in sports and regular play by his inability to see in three dimensions, Billy retreated into a dreamy childhood and lonely adolescence. When his father bought him a used guitar for his thirteenth Christmas, Billy carried his new companion wherever he went, practicing his father's hillbilly ballads, his mother's British and Baptist hymns, and the pop and country songs he heard on the radio. On Saturdays he'd catch a ride into Chester to the Marcus Hook Theater to attend the western movie matinees, especially the ones starring his idol, singing cowboy Gene Autry. By the time Billy was fifteen, he was known around Booth's Corner as a pretty good country singer and yodeler, even though he was too shy to get up in front of a crowd of strangers.

If it seems odd that a kid born in Michigan and raised near Philadelphia took so fervidly to Southern rural music, consider that what we call "country" was essentially a big-city product to begin with. (A pejorative early-twentieth-century term, "hillbilly," was affixed to the music by record executive Ralph Peer around 1926.) Though antebellum folk songs by string bands and Appalachian fiddlers sold well in the early 1920s, the first country music star was a New York light opera singer named Marion Try Slaughter, who on a lark in 1925, after hearing an Okeh recording of a rough, drawling singer-guitarist named Henry Whittier singing "The Wreck of the Southern Old 97," decided to duplicate Whittier's homey, rustic style—only more hammy. Taking the names of two Texas towns near where he'd lived as a boy, he called himself Vernon Dalhart and rerecorded the song under the less-unwieldy title, "The Wreck of the Old 97," for Victor Records. But it was the flipside, "The Prisoner's Song," that ended up selling at least seven million platters and establishing a fertile field of country music. Another early, though less popular, artist was Emmett Miller, a minstrel singer who recorded in Manhattan with a studio band dubbed the Georgia Crackers, which included future bandleaders Tommy and Jimmy Dorsey on trombone and saxophone, respectively.

Not until Ralph Peer discovered Jimmie Rodgers in 1927 did contemporary Southern music by a blue-collar artist cross over in a big way to a general American audience. Rodgers, a consumptive Mississippi railroad man who copied Emmett Miller's gravelly yodel, established the chaps-and-Stetson image of the singing cowboy late in his short career, and when Rodgers died in 1933, Oklahoma telegraph operator Gene Autry stepped into his boots and recorded songs like "Methodist Pie" in a voice so similar that buyers were initially confused. Gradually Autry found his own style—and young Bill Haley found Autry.

In the summer of 1940, as soon as he finished the eighth grade, Billy quit school for good and took a job at a local factory. He never considered being a professional musician until three years later when he was asked to play at the weekly farmer's market at the Booth's Corner Auction Mart, a huge barn just down the road from his house. Standing on a couple of old wooden tables pushed together to form a stage under a big oak tree, he drew a crowd singing popular songs like "You Are My Sunshine" and "Has Anybody Seen My Gal." Word quickly spread to surrounding communities that there was a kid at the Auction Mart who sang like Gene Autry.

As he became more confident onstage, Billy developed an easy manner and the corny patter required of any working hillbilly artist. Within a few months, when his pay for a half-hour's performance went from one dollar to five, he drove into Philadelphia to visit a hoedown haberdasher named Rodeo Ben and buy a ten-gallon hat, a pair of white leather boots, and a bright red western suit with all the trimmings. He played his first major gig in the fall of 1943, opening at the local Radio Park for singing cowboy Roy Rogers and the Sons of the Pioneers in front of 10,000 people. He promptly quit his defense plant job.

Near the end of 1945 or very early '46, Haley joined Shorty Cook's Down Homers, a string band well known around the Midwest because of their weekly performances on the *Hoosier Hop* radio show. It aired live on Saturday nights from powerhouse WOWO in Fort Wayne, Indiana, and was replayed via transcription discs three nights later around the country on the Blue (later ABC) radio network. Though he got to yodel and sing a little, Bill was mostly confined to playing rhythm guitar and harmonizing in the background, but he considered his time with the Down Homers the genesis of his career. Talking with Canadian disc jockey Red Robinson in Vancouver twenty years later, he said, "The beginning for Bill Haley—let's really go back, now—was ...1946 to be exact.... In those days I was a Swiss yodeler."

On his earliest known recording, a 1946 radio aircheck with the Down Homers, Haley sang "She Taught Me to Yodel." He also took his first profes-

Young country crooner Bill Haley's first publicity photo, in 1946, billed him as "The Rambling Yodeler."

sional photo, as "Bill Haley the Rambling Yodeler," with his white Stetson tilted like a halo on the back of his head and a thick spit curl plastered over the right side of his forehead to distract people's attention from his crippled, slightly crooked left eye. The spit curl, known also as a kiss curl, later became his trademark, as visually distinctive as the gardenia in jazz songbird Billie Holiday's hair.

It wasn't long before he got into a salary dispute with Shorty Cook and split with a couple of other members to form the Range Drifters, made up of a bass, two guitars, and a fiddle. Despite their several appearances on the *National Barn Dance* on Chicago superstation WLS and Haley defeating RCA Victor recording artist Elton Britt to win the 1946 Indiana State Fair yodeling championship, the Range Drifters soon found themselves trapped on the grueling honky-tonk circuit, traveling bone-wearying distances in their car each night with the bass fiddle strapped to the top, living on canned beans and coffee and relying on their fans to supply amenities like cigarettes and alcohol.

As the quartet trundled around the country from New England to New Orleans to Dallas to the oil fields of Oklahoma, Haley had a chance to listen to music he'd never heard before. G.I.s returning from World War II were looking for something different, something more upbeat and exhilarating, and they were finding it in California's hillbilly boogie, Texas's western swing, New Orleans' rumba-flavored piano R&B, Chicago's electrified Mississippi guitar blues, and St. Louis's swing jazz. Haley noticed that every region of the country had its own rhythms, its own musical strains that weren't being heard regularly on the national radio networks. He wasn't performing in these styles himself, but they soaked into his fingers, his skin; the exposure to such a rainbow of American music would later be his only consolation for that ragged year on the road.

When the Range Drifters finally drifted apart in Oklahoma in late summer of 1946, Bill was so destitute that he had to sing his way back home in medicine shows and roadside diners. His final humiliation came when he hopped a freight train to Fort Wayne to beg Shorty Cook for his old job back with the Down Homers. Cook bluntly told him that with the war over, young singers like him were a dime a dozen. In one last pang of generosity he shoved forty dollars into the pocket of Bill's dirty shirt and sent the half-starved twenty-one-year-old cowboy crooner back home to Pennsylvania.

As Haley said later, "I needed to get a steady job, forget my foolish ideas [about a singing career], and accomplish something that was real.... All I could think of is, I'm a failure and now everybody is going to know it."

Through an old friend he landed a job as a radio personality (the term "disc jockey" wasn't yet in play) at a New Hampshire station, then moved in early 1947 to larger operations, first in Connecticut and then in Lebanon, Pennsylvania, not far from home. He married a Booth's Corner girl, Dottie Crowe, and soon had a baby on the way. Whenever he had the chance, he'd liven up his radio show by playing some of the so-called "race" records by black artists he'd picked up in New Orleans and St. Louis, but the station managers always complained.

Then one day he heard that a new station, WPWA, was going on the air back home in Chester. It was a small dawn-to-dusk broadcaster, but its 250 watts would reach all the factory towns up and down the Delaware Valley, including Philadelphia itself. When Bill rushed home to interview for the job of musical director, he offered the owner, Lou Pollar, a proposal: Since the area's many blacks, blue-collar whites, and eastern European immigrants were being ignored by the larger stations, why not program all types of music during the day to appeal to them—polkas, ethnic folk songs, R&B, hillbilly, Dixieland, bebop? Pollar gave him a counterproposal: He'd go along with this format if Bill Haley himself sold advertising, wrote and delivered the commercials, hosted some of the shows and hired people to do the others, gathered together a musical library, announced the sports and weather, then grabbed a broom and swept up the studio at the end of the day. That was just fine with Bill. He took the job.

The long days at WPWA gave him a deeper insight into what folks wanted to hear. For example, after he inaugurated an all-black music show called *Judge Rhythm's Court*, hosted two hours daily by a white man who spoke in a black dialect, Bill learned that many of the listeners calling in or sending cards to request rhythm and blues records were young whites. He also took a liking to the show's noisy theme song, "Rock the Joint," newly recorded by local bandleader Jimmy Preston for Gotham Records in Philadelphia.

At the same time, he was hosting his own live *Western Swing Hour* that put him at the center of Philadelphia's country music market. He assembled a WPWA studio group called the 4 Aces of Western Swing, featuring two guitars, a bass, and an accordion. In early 1948 he added a fiddle and steel guitar to bring the band more in line with Pee Wee King's Golden West Cowboys, who were having a huge hit at the time with "Tennessee Waltz." One day the lead guitarist, James "Slim" Allsman, came to work with a new electric Gibson Premier. Though the electric guitar was still unacceptable to most Nashville producers, Bill liked the way it fattened up the sound of his band.

His job at WPWA also reacquainted him with a local hustler named Jack Howard whom he'd known at Radio Park several years earlier. Howard was now an impresario with his own country music publishing company and tiny label, Cowboy Records, whose discs he distributed himself around the Delaware Valley, lugging boxes of 78s from store to store and leaving them on

The 4 Aces of Western Swing were accordionist Al Constantine, guitarists Tex King and Bill Haley, and bassist Julian "Bashful Barney" Barnard.

consignment. Because he owed a few debts or favors to a Philadelphia crime family, he also supplied royalty-free singles for the Mafia-owned jukeboxes in the area and in several Midwestern cities.

Unlike most company owners, Howard didn't pay artists to record; they financed their own sessions and paid him to manufacture their recordings. So Bill Haley hired him to press up a couple of things the 4 Aces of Western Swing had recorded at WPWA's studio, including "Four Leaf Clover Blues," which Haley had written during his time with the Down Homers. Though he paid Jack Howard twenty-five cents for each record pressed, he was satisfied with the arrangement at first because he could spin them on the radio and sell them for a small profit at his nightly personal appearances. Howard's five thousand "extras" for mob jukeboxes provided even more free publicity. As a bonus, another local country singer named Pete "Pancake" Newman covered Bill's "Four Leaf Clover Blues" for RCA Victor.

But all this activity—running the radio station from sunup to sundown and performing in honky-tonks up and down the Delaware River late into the night—barely made him enough money to break even. He became chronically exhausted and depressed, started drinking at his shows, and ignored his marriage. At one point he got so drunk at a dingy, worn-down joint in Chester called Luke's Musical Bar that he smashed his fist through the bathroom wall. His hand was so swollen that he couldn't play his guitar for a month, and permanent damage prevented him from ever being a competent lead guitarist thereafter. He disbanded the 4 Aces of Western Swing, thinking maybe he should go back to the factory and give up his dreams of being a music star.

It was during this dark period that another local song publisher came to the radio station one day, introduced himself, and asked Haley to spin one of his company's latest songs. He also offered Haley twenty-five bucks to record a couple of other songs he owned. The visitor was Jimmy Myers, president of a one-man operation called Myers Music, and the two songs he brought with him were lightweight hillbilly items—later released on Center Records out of Maryland under the name Johnny Clifton and His String Band—that only a handful of record collectors remembers today. But the meeting began a beneficial relationship for both men. Five years later Myers would bring Bill Haley the song of his life.

CHAPTER 5

CALLING ALL COMETS

One day at the radio station in late 1949, Slim Allsman, Haley's former guitarist, showed up with a couple of musicians who wanted to talk to him about putting together a new group. One was a twenty-four-year-old steel guitarist and fiddler named Billy Williamson. The other was Johnny Grande (pronounced *gran-dee*), a nineteen-year-old classically trained pianist and accordion player. Though close as brothers, the two were an almost comical contrast—Mutt and Jeff without the startling difference in height. Williamson was slightly heavyset with a jowly, jolly Irish face and receding hairline—a used-car-salesman kind of guy—whereas Grande was an intense, skinny Italian kid with jug ears and bushy black eyebrows. "I remember the way Billy introduced me to Haley," Grande wrote in a 1957 magazine. "'Johnny can play piano and accordion—pops, western, or Dixie. He's had eight years of classical musical education, too. And in eight years one can't help learning something…even this guy.'" Haley wasn't interested. They had very little experience as stage performers, and besides, he didn't want the worries of leading another band. He said no thanks.

But when Grande and Williamson showed up a few nights later at Luke's Musical Bar and talked with him again, Haley was in a warmer mood. He appreciated their enthusiasm about his ideas and their willingness to try something new. On a more practical level, he needed somebody like Grande who was musically educated enough to notate arrangements off the top of his head. As Grande remembers it, Haley told them, "All my life I've been looking for something I haven't yet found in music. I've always thought if I could get together with some guys who felt the same way I did, we might work it out." At the end of their impromptu meeting, the three shook hands and declared themselves equal partners, though Haley, by dint of his experience and local celebrity, would have the last word. They dubbed their new group Bill Haley and the Saddlemen.

Born in South Philadelphia on January 14, 1930, Johnny Grande had been taking accordion lessons since he was seven. When his family moved to the suburbs in the mid-forties, he began playing in various country bands for extra money on weekends over the objection of his father. "I wasn't working steady with anybody at that time, just any band that needed an accordion player," he told Lee Cotten. Most people don't associate Italian-American musicians with country music, or with black music for that matter, but in eastern Pennsylvania, New Jersey, and New York they had a tradition of playing in hillbilly and R&B bands. Over the next several years, more than half of the various members of Bill Haley's band would be Italians.

Grande's presence on the accordion showed the influence of Pee Wee King's Golden West Cowboys on the new Saddlemen. King was a Polish-American accordionist from Wisconsin, born Frank Kuczynski, who began with a polka band in 1929 and gradually crossed over into the polished country jazz of Bob Wills & His Texas Playboys, as well as the disciplined vocal harmonies of the Sons of the Pioneers. Throughout most of the 1940s his Golden West Cowboys were regulars on *The Grand Ole Opry*, where he popularized the accordion as a country instrument. King gained national fame after he left the show in 1948 and began a string of hits, including the original "Tennessee Waltz." Grande, however, would restrict his accordion to live shows; in the studio he played only piano on the Saddlemen and early Comets recordings.

William F. "Billy" Williamson was born in the Schuylkill River town of Conshohocken, just northwest of Philadelphia, on February 9, 1925, and grew up a few miles upriver in Norristown. He taught himself to play lap steel guitar, and by the time he joined Bill Haley he was playing a cream-colored, top-of-the-line Gibson Console Grande.

The technique of sliding a steel bolt with the left hand across the strings of a regular, Spanish-style guitar to get a slurred effect was created around 1895 by an eleven-year-old Honolulu boy named Joseph Kekuku. By age eighteen Kekuku had fine-tuned his own unmistakable style, laying his guitar face up on his lap and using a smooth steel bar he'd fashioned in shop class. He later toured the United States, made the first steel guitar recordings for Thomas Edison, and taught his method to other musicians before his early death. In the late 1920s, with the invention of the metal-body guitar with built-in resonators to increase the volume, the so-called Hawaiian steel guitar truly became steel. That in turn created feedback problems when electrical amplification arrived a couple of years later, prompting manufacturers to redesign the instrument as a solid body that fit more comfortably in the lap. As they added necks to provide more strings and different tunings, the steel guitar became so unwieldy that legs also had to be added. Though it was now a standing console, the name lap steel remained.

The steel guitar had entered popular hillbilly music in early 1928 when E. T. Cozzens played one on several Jimmie Rodgers recordings. The first notable soloist was Leon McAuliffe, who joined Bob Wills & His Texas Playboys in 1935 and turned his own "Steel Guitar Rag" into one of the band's biggest crowd pleasers. By the late forties the major hillbilly sellers like Eddy Arnold, Tennessee Ernie Ford, and Hank Williams were accompanied by steel guitarists, each one a distinctive voice. Though Billy Williamson claimed to favor Arnold's Nashville-based Little Roy Wiggins, he seemed more clearly influenced by two experimental, high-wire-walking California pickers, Joaquin Murphy from Spade Cooley's band and Wes "Speedy" West from Tennessee Ernie Ford's studio group.

Haley, Grande, and Williamson rehearsed nearly every day in WPWA's basement and experimented with various styles and syncopations. They worked out ways to make their three instruments sound fuller together, doubling notes, filling every available space, wasting nothing. And as they stumbled onto things they liked, Grande jotted them down on charts. Since all three played more than one instrument, they could try many different permutations. Grande went back and forth between the piano and his accordion. Williamson could step away from his steel guitar, pick up the fiddle, grab one of Haley's guitars, or fill in on the bass. Haley played guitar and bass and dabbled on the fiddle.

According to Grande, "We took any bookings we could get: lodge dances, banquets, weddings, little joints that called themselves nightclubs. But the important thing was that we rehearsed in the studio every day for two years.... One of the [WPWA] engineers gave us a big assist by putting our trial runs on tape and playing them back so we could study them.... Always, we were always looking for something different. We'd take a standard, like 'Ida [Sweet as Apple

Cider],' and play it every way we could think of...fast, slow, loud, soft, hillbilly, waltz, Dixie, progressive." One breakthrough came when they were listening to a couple of Count Basie records. "Since we didn't have brasses, we fooled around with the strings, trying to get the same effect, trying to build volume. Haley, with the bass, discovered that when he plucked the strings in the accepted way, it came out 'rrom-*pahhh*.' If he back-slapped them, it changed the accent to '*rrrroom*-pah.' That's how the heavy backbeat became the basic form in our rock 'n' roll."

The four-string double bass viol—more simply called the bass—became an important part of what the Saddlemen were looking for. A member of the violin family with a history going back to sixteenth-century Europe, the bass didn't become a soloist's instrument until Domenico Dragonetti, a friend of Beethoven's, popularized it in the early 1800s. The bass was played with a bow and, occasionally, by finger-plucking the strings. But by the end of the century, a few basses fell into the hands of New Orleans black string bands, whose players had already developed a street style of thumping rhythm on the so-called "washtub bass," a common homemade instrument with roots in West and Central Africa. These "folk artists" had turned metal washtubs or buckets upside down, punched a hole in the middle of the bottom, poked a broomstick into the hole, attached a cord between the metal and the top of the wooden stick, and drawn it taut. They got a resonant sound from the tub by pressing the cord against the upper part of the stick with one hand and slapping the lower part of the cord with the other. Probably the first professional musician to successfully transfer the washtub slap style to the double bass viol was New Orleans jazzman George "Pops" Foster, who was using the technique as early as 1918. Foster also developed what became the standard stance for playing jazz bass: holding the instrument upright instead of leaning it toward himself, as the bass was played by classical musicians, and using his left thumb along with his fingers in order to tighten the strings against the fingerboard, creating bigger overtones. However, since acoustic recording couldn't pick up the bass's low frequencies very well, bands used tubas in the studio until electrical recording widened the range of sound that engineers could work with. Probably the first major star to introduce the heavy bass sound to a pop audience was Paul Whiteman, a white bandleader who dominated the record charts in the 1920s.

Writer Harvey Pekar, in *Down Beat* magazine, credited Oscar Pettiford for moving the bass out front as a percussive instrument in an early 1940s Dizzy

Gillespie band that played bebop, at that time a new jazz form with erratic or internal rhythms: "Since the drummers no longer marked off a steady pulse with the bass drum, the time-keeping duties fell heavily on the bassist. He became more aggressive—taking charge of the rhythm section—for his playing was now the foundation of the performance."

Though Bill Haley's dance music was the antithesis of bebop, this "aggressive" bass playing was exactly what he was looking for. In late 1949 he found a local bass player named Albert Piccirilli, better known as Al Rex, who could slap a steady beat on the strings of his instrument, sing when needed, and do comedy routines between songs. The band was finally complete. And according to Grande, they were all obsessed with rhythm.

"Time after time Bill Haley would say, 'We've got to get [the crowd] on their feet. Make them move. Make them feel that rhythm.' We talked about it constantly, for this, we knew, was the biggest problem any musician faced. America had quit dancing. That period when the vocalist was the top attraction had brought an end of the big band and big dance hall. Kids listened instead of danced. The entertainment tax had killed off dancing in nightclubs—and the jobs with the clubs."

By now music publisher Jimmy Myers was looking to get more of his songs on wax. Since small record labels were always looking for new product that wouldn't cost them anything, he was willing to pay artists to record his material and then offer the results to whatever company would release them. As Myers saw it, the money he spent was an investment in the songs he owned. If they weren't out in the marketplace, they couldn't be played on the radio or on the jukeboxes and wouldn't be heard by more successful artists looking for new songs. Having already gotten Haley a one-off record on the tiny Center label, Myers hired the Saddlemen to record four of his western swing tunes, co-written under his pen name, Jimmy DeKnight. He placed four tracks with Atlantic Records, an unsuccessful New York jazz label that was looking to spread out into something new and hadn't yet fixed on the rhythm and blues that would later make its fortune. These records didn't sell very well or put any money into the group's pockets, but they made it easier for Myers to promote the Saddlemen to clubs around Philadelphia.

When Communist North Korean troops unexpectedly invaded South Korea in June 1950, the United States hastily mobilized and spearheaded a United Nations campaign to stop them. The naval shipyards on the Delaware River came alive almost overnight, and as ships were tugged in for repairs and upgrading before heading off to the Far East, their crews jammed into Philadelphia's clubs, looking for a last good time. They found it at the Spigot Cafe, where the Saddle-Men—as one ad spelled it—were booked in for a two-week stand. Playing what they now called "cowboy jive," the group was such a crowd-rouser that the Twin Bar, a bustling dinner and dance place across the Delaware River in Gloucester, New Jersey, hired them for a two-week gig that lasted for the next year and a half. It was there that Bill Haley and his group perfected their proto–rock 'n' roll style.

As John W. Haley and John von Hoelle described it in their biography of Bill Haley, "At the Twin Bar about ten o'clock every Friday and Saturday night, the Saddlemen would stop playing their country-western music. Bill would then announce to the crowd with a big grin, 'All you hillbillies out there gotta go home now, 'cause we're gonna play a little something we call Cowboy Jive. It's a mixture of western swing, Dixieland, and hard-edge blues. And we're the only band crazy enough to play it.'" Then they cranked up their two amplifiers and let the music vibrate off the walls. "As the older generation and the lovers of pure country music made for the doors with their hands over their ears, the young people would pack the large room. Within ten minutes, the place rocked with the craziest music this side of the moon." Haley himself would later describe their show at the Twin Bar as "a hand-clappin', stompin' sort of a semi-gospel type music." One of the songs they played was "Rock the Joint," the R&B theme song from *Judge Rhythm's Court*.

By now the group had acquired a new manager and business partner. Haley had first asked Jimmy Myers if he'd be interested in managing them, but Myers claimed that his other enterprises, especially his music publishing company, were already taking up too much of his time. So Haley turned to his friend James "Lord Jim" Ferguson, a part-time sports commentator at WPWA who published a free entertainment newsletter distributed to all the clubs and restaurants around the Chester area. An ex-carny, Ferguson chewed large cigars and pushed himself into other people's faces. In many ways he resembled—physically and otherwise—his old pal Colonel Tom Parker, who at the time was managing country singer Hank Snow. Haley knew that Lord Jim had a reputation as a hustler, but he considered it a protective asset in the shadowy, unscrupulous world of nighttime entertainment.

Johnny Grande recalled that Ferguson had already taken an interest in the band. "We were his hobby—until eventually we took up so much of his time, we asked him if he would let us *be* his business." They officially made him a fourth partner in the Saddlemen. "Jim is the one who foraged around, got us bookings, guided us through the times when we didn't fit anywhere," said Grande. Lord Jim also gave them two pieces of valuable advice: First, forget the "cowboy jive" image, ditch the hillbilly duds, and start wearing tailored suits; second, since young people seemed to be the most receptive to what the Saddlemen were playing, the band should volunteer to do free gigs at high schools around the area and get the kids talking about them.

Grande recalled that their many free daytime shows at high school assemblies were inconvenient for musicians already dead tired from late-night gigs, "but it was the smartest thing we ever tried. The kids taught us. We tried our experiments on them. When their shoulders started moving, their feet tapping and their hands clapping, we knew that particular tune or style was worth keeping in the act." One of the first things Haley learned from these high school programs was that the kids didn't care much for the train-rhythm boogie-woogie in the Saddlemen repertoire. "We found the rhythm too fast [for them] and the idea of boogie-woogie was passé with the kids. It was old hat," Haley later told British disc jockey Roger Scott. "They didn't want to hear this, you know, they wanted something new."

As word got around, the packed shows at the Twin Bar caught the attention of a local record company owner named Dave Miller. In June 1951 Miller called Haley at the radio station and asked him if he was interested in doing a record. Miller had just got back from visiting his distributors down South, where everybody was talking about an R&B record on the Chicago-based Chess label called "Rocket 88" by Jackie Brenston and His Delta Cats. The loping blues shuffle had been cut three months earlier in Memphis, at Sun Studio, where many bluesmen like B.B. King and Howlin' Wolf recorded. Despite the Delta Cats name on the label, the band was actually the Kings of Rhythm, led by a Mississippi piano player named Ike Turner. On the trip up to Memphis, Willie Kizart, the band's guitarist, had busted his amplifier speaker. In the studio it create a ragged buzz that turned out to be the most distinctive element of the record.

Miller was so captivated by the record's raw power that he wanted to make a cover version for the local white market. "He came to me," Haley told writer Ken Terry, "and said, 'I want to make a record of you, and we'll put it out, but we won't use any pictures, because we don't want people to know if you're black or white.'" He offered the Saddlemen a one-off deal to record "Rocket 88" and one of Haley's own songs for the B-side: an advance payment for the session ($25 to Haley and $15 for each sideman), royalties on records sold, and no jukebox giveaways.

In WPWA's basement the group sat down and listened to "Rocket 88" a few times on a phonograph, then began working out an arrangement. Haley sang and played rhythm guitar, Grande sat at the piano, Williamson played steel guitar, and Al Rex thumped on the bass. When they finally had something they liked, they went upstairs to record an acetate demo in the radio studio. Haley delivered it to Miller the next day. The loose-jointed performance—a mix of 1930s boogie-woogie and hillbilly swing—sounded fine, Miller told him, except he wanted a bigger backbeat that would make it jump out of the jukeboxes. He also wanted a more dominant lead electric guitar, like the one on the Jackie Brenston record. Haley called Robert Scaltrito, who occasionally sat in with the band at clubs, because he could play in the swinging, single-note style of Eldon Shamblin, the electric guitarist from Bob Wills & His Texas Playboys. The next day the band went back into the studio and cut the first modern Bill Haley record. Al Rex later told John Swenson, "I had this old bass fiddle that did not have a soundpost. When I used to slap it you didn't hear no tone, all you used to hear was *clickety-clickety-clickety-click*. Dave Miller said, 'That's what I want to hear.' He said, 'Put the microphone on that bass. Let's get that sound.'" Miller released the song in July on his new Holiday label. It eventually sold ten thousand copies and prompted Miller to sign the Saddlemen to a contract.

Years later, several people around Miller claimed that he was the first record company owner to encourage a white singer to sing like a Negro. But Bill Haley, though he used R&B rhythms, never sounded black. On his records he vocally resembled Gene Autry but without Autry's Oklahoma accent. In fact, Haley had no accent to speak of. Growing up in northern blue-collar suburbs had flattened his voice into a generic Midwestern English, lacking any of the inflections of regional dialects, black or white. And to his credit Haley never affected any.

What Dave Miller had recognized was that rhythm and blues had such a visceral appeal that, given the chance to be heard at nightclubs or on café jukeboxes, it could cross the color line, at least with young people whose formative years had been World War II, when much of white America's animus toward blacks had been temporarily diverted toward Japs and Nazis.

Miller may have been more receptive to black music than Americans his own age because he was a German immigrant—born David Kleiber around

1901—who'd come to America in the 1930s and joined the U.S. military during the war. He owned a record distribution company with his brother Paul and their father Al, but he supplemented the family business by toting a portable disc recorder to churches and high schools around town to aurally transcribe choirs, weddings, bar mitzvahs, and marching bands. As Paul Miller later recalled, "Dave would go out and pound the street all day, and would get an order for three hundred [records] from a high school." By 1947 they began hearing complaints from local jukebox operators that the bigger companies weren't keeping up with the demand for regional records that working-class people wanted to hear. "One day, Dave said to me, 'You know, we should get into pressing [our own] records.'" The brothers used their G.I. loans to order two record presses from California, named their company Palda Records (for Paul, Al, and Dave), and began recording pop and race music. Their first successful act was the Ferko String Band, a rowdy aggregation of anywhere from a few dozen to several hundred street musicians—mostly banjo players but also many non-string contributors like glockenspielists, saxophonists, and tuba players—who were (and still are) an annual favorite at Philadelphia's New Year's Day Mummers Parade. According to Paul Miller, "We used to take them up to [radio station] WIP for recording. We'd put a bunch of those guys in there in warm weather in their undershirts and it was something else."

By late 1947 Miller had sold enough copies of the Ferko String Band's noisy version of the then-hot "(I'm Looking Over) A Four-Leaf Clover" around town that King Records, a nationally distributed indie label in Cincinnati, purchased the master for a wider release. Now that the Ferko boys were hot, Miller put a call out for original songs. A trio of writers, including Max C. Freedman, responded with a tune called "Heartbreaker." Within several weeks, the Ferko String Band's new Palda single was a national seller, thanks to a national musicians' strike that crippled the major record industry through most of 1948 and gave storefront operations the chance to fill the void. Then the famous Andrews Sisters, backed only by a non-union harmonica group, harmonized a hit cover version for Decca. By the time Dave Miller found Bill Haley three years later, Palda Records was thriving. He could make all the records he needed and get them out to where they had to go.

Unfortunately, the next couple of singles by the Saddlemen went nowhere. Despite the relative success of "Rocket 88," they slipped back into making records that were more hillbilly boogie than rhythm and blues, probably because Haley was still skeptical about how much R&B he could get away with.

Playing for drunken sailors at the Twin Bar or for rhythm-crazy kids at high schools was one thing, but making recordings for the general country and western listener was another thing altogether. As he told Ken Terry, "This was an era when there was very strong prejudice in music. If you sang what they called race music, why, you did only that.... I did ['Rocket 88'] out of stupidity. I just didn't realize what I was doing."

Haley had also become enamored of Hank Williams, currently the hottest act in country music. "My influence in the country field came from Hank Williams, largely because of the good songs he wrote, the heart songs and blues," he later told Arnold Shaw. He was so taken by Williams's "Cold Cold Heart" that when a couple of Miller's composers wrote him a ballad called "Icy Heart," he was raring to record it at his next session.

For the B-side, either Jack Howard or Miller suggested that the Saddlemen record "Rock the Joint," the Jimmy Preston number that always went over well when they played it at the Twin Bar. After Wynonie Harris's "Good Rockin' Tonight" brought "rock" back into the vernacular of the R&B world, three black Philadelphia musicians had retooled an unsuccessful 1947 Nelson Alexander song called "Rock the Voot," titled it "Rock the Joint," and jammed it with lyrics about blowing down walls, gettin' high as a kite, and jitterbugging all night long "until the law come knockin' at the door." When they handed it to Preston in 1949, he and his band turned the song into a raucous party, complete with hooting hell-raisers and a shrieking saxophone—a real jukebox-rattler.

Haley loved performing the song, but it was a goof, a novelty whose main purpose was warming up the crowds and letting the Saddlemen jump around and mug as part of their stage show. It had entered their live act as an accident. As he later told *TV-Radio Mirror*, "[At the Twin Bar] I went into ['Rock the Joint'], hitting it with our *rrrroom*-pah beat instead of the [shuffle] way [Preston recorded it]. Billy and Johnny started to laugh and joined in. Al Rex hit it on the bass. We really got a kick out of it ourselves. It was our private joke. Then I looked around—and so help me, people were dancing. I turned to the guys and asked, 'What on earth did I do?'"

By now the Saddlemen had added a new full-time member. In late 1951 Al Rex quit because he didn't like the idea of being the group's only hired hand. His replacement was Marshall Lytle (rhymes with *bridle*), a teenage singer-guitarist who hosted his own early morning radio show on WVCH, Chester's other country station besides WPWA. Born just outside Asheville, North Carolina, on September 1, 1933, Lytle had moved to Chester as a boy when his

The Saddlemen in 1952 were (clockwise from bottom) Bill Haley, bassist Marshall Lytle, steel guitarist Billy Williamson, and accordionist Johnny Grande.

parents came north to work in the shipyards during the war. He had never played the bass, but Haley, who knew Lytle from shows around town, assured him, "I'll teach you—it's easy."

As Lytle recalls, "That afternoon I went to his house and he taught me how to slap the bass fiddle. Bill was quite a bass player himself. He taught me the basics that I needed to know. Sometimes I'd hit some sharp notes or flat ones, but the slap beat was the thing that Bill was most interested in having me hone my talents on.... I went out and bought a bass fiddle that afternoon and went to work with him that night [at the Twin Bar]. It was that quick." For the first few weeks his fingers bled. "We didn't have amplified instruments, except for the steel guitar and Bill's rhythm guitar. And Bill was always telling us to play it loud."

Another valuable, though part-time, addition to the Saddlemen was guitarist Danny Cedrone, a dapper man with a pencil mustache. Cedrone was never a member of Haley's band because he had his own full-time group, the Esquire Boys, but Haley asked him to play on some of his recordings. Born Donato Joseph Cedrone on June 20, 1920, in Jamesville, New York, he grew up in a large musical family in South Philadelphia. According to his grandson Dan Vanore, Cedrone's mother taught him how to play guitar. Along with the Neapolitan love songs of his childhood, he developed an early interest in hillbilly music, particularly the jazz-inflected work of Eldon Shamblin, an Oklahoma boy who had laid down a series of bold, electrified solos with Bob Wills's Texas Playboys as early as 1941. Coincidentally, one of Shamblin's main inspirations had been a Philadelphia Italian named Salvatore Massaro, jazz's first virtuoso guitarist, who had grown up only a few blocks from Cedrone's neighborhood. Classically trained as a violinist and banjo player, Massaro—using the name Eddie Lang—had begun recording with the guitar in 1923, before the introduction of the electrical microphone allowed its light strings to be properly heard. After Massaro's early death in 1933 at age 31, his high-speed yet melodic single-string solos became the standard for countless jazz, country, and R&B guitarists.

Cedrone played one of the classic jazz guitars, the Gibson ES-300, an electrified hollowbody popular for its warm tones. With its *zaftig*, feminine-shaped body—seventeen inches thick—and a neck as fat as the barrel end of a Louisville Slugger, it was one of the hardest guitars to play, yet he seemed to have no problem darting his fingers around its frets. After Cedrone backed up a Bill Haley duet with Loretta Glendenning ("I'm Crying") on a 1951 session for Holiday Records, Haley asked him to record with the Saddlemen on their upcoming session.

Though Haley rewrote some of the lyrics of "Rock the Joint" to appeal to his country dance audience, he kept the song's R&B hook because he had begun to sense the power of the masculine, hyperactive word "rock": "We're gonna *rock*—rock this joint—we're gonna *rock*—rock this joint—we're gonna *rock*—rock this joint—we're gonna rock this joint tonight!" No doubt part of the allure of "Rocket 88" had been that "rocket" sounded like "rock it," as in "we're gonna rock it." At the same time, rocket carried its own cachet. Though it went way back to the fourteenth-century Italian *rocchetta*—a paper or metal cylinder that could be fired into the air with gunpowder—rocket was a shiny and futuristic word to Americans in the early fifties. The Nazi V1 and V2 rockets that had been designed to fall indiscriminately on London during World War II were now being retrofitted by German émigré scientists for America's explorations into space. Washington propaganda and Madison Avenue hype had whetted a civilian fascination for what was being touted as "space age" technology. Detroit's automobile designers had begun using rocket motifs on new cars to suggest speed and ultra-modernity. "Rocket 88," in fact, was a paean to the 1950 Hydra-Matic Drive V-8 Oldsmobile 88, advertised as "the lowest priced car with a 'rocket engine'" under its "sleek Futuramic hood."

According to Haley, "We changed ["Rock the Joint"] from a shuffle to a 2/4 beat, and we added to this the flavor of the old-time swing bands." As Marshall Lytle slapped his bass, Miller balanced it high in the mix to make the percussive clicking drive the rhythm. But the most stunning moments of the song came after the second verse, when Danny Cedrone got the nod to deliver a fleet-fingered eight-bar solo that was almost stupefying in its energy. It was such a great execution, in fact, that he would repeat it, note for note, two years later on "Rock Around the Clock."

Miller released "Rock the Joint"/"Icy Heart" on a new label, Essex Records, in April 1952. The single became an instant hit on local jukeboxes, the public's voting booths in the music popularity sweepstakes. Whether café and club customers were playing "Rock the Joint" or "Icy Heart," or whether kids were punching "Rock the Joint" to irritate older people, didn't matter. All Miller cared about was how often the jukebox distributors ordered new 78s to replace the ones being worn out by the grinding jukebox needle pressure. Now all he needed was some airplay.

In July he sent Haley and Lord Jim Ferguson on a promotional tour of major radio stations around the eastern part of the country, carrying a cache of $25 U.S. Savings Bonds to give to disc jockeys as a customary token of gratitude. Most of their stops were country music stations because "Icy Heart" was the more commercial side. But as Haley later told Ken Terry, "I...got to Nashville with hopes of going on *The Grand Ole Opry*, and I got a phone call from Dave Miller in the hotel room that evening telling me to get off 'Icy Heart' and get on 'Rock the Joint' because that was hitting." The news disappointed him at first.

"Here I was with the sideburns, cowboy boots, and almost ten years of promoting myself as a country and western singer." The record went on to sell seventy-five thousand copies and become popular enough in Chicago that a black jazz club inexplicably hired the Saddlemen for a week, following bebop trumpeter Dizzy Gillespie. The audiences walked out on them and the club sent them packing before the week was out, but clearly Haley and the boys were onto something.

He began writing "rock" songs, beginning with a whimsical trifle called "Rockin' Chair on the Moon," featuring a chorus—"I got a *rock—rock—rock*in' chair on the moon"—accompanied by Williamson whizzing sci-fi notes into the stratosphere. For Danny Cedrone's Esquire Boys he wrote "Rock-A-Beatin' Boogie," with its exhortation to "Rock rock rock, everybody, roll roll roll, everybody." And then, for the Saddlemen's next session near the end of 1952, he wrote his own first modern rock 'n' roll record, "Real Rock Drive."

What distinguished this session was that for the first time he used a drummer, Billy Gussak, who had worked enough with jazz artists that he could accommodate himself to the group's tight bass-driven arrangements by playing sparingly until the song needed a sudden burst of energy or a rim shot to accent the beat. Gussak's presence finally ended Haley's ambivalence about which direction his band should take. From now on, any gesture toward Nashville—the hub of the traditional country music business, where drums were *verboten*—was out of the question. The Saddlemen were taking their cues from Los Angeles, which had been in the throes of a drum-powered country boogie boom since the late 1940s, when Tennessee Ernie Ford's "Shot Gun Boogie," featuring Roy Harte's prominent 2/4 snare drum pops, sold a million copies. Many Southern California country artists, such as Spade Cooley and the Maddox Brothers & Rose, were Okie migrants steeped in western swing from Texas, where Bob Wills & His Texas Playboys had been using drums since the late 1930s. Anyone doubting the California influence on Haley need only hear the opening of "Real Rock Drive"—a repetitive three-note riff taken directly from Tennessee Ernie Ford's 1951 "Kissin' Bug Boogie"—that ran through most of the recording, played in tandem on the amped-up steel and electric guitars.

Though Haley hired local drummers for his live shows, he would use only Gussak at recording sessions over the next several years. A Russian Jew whose father had studied violin at the Odessa Conservatory, Gussak himself had been classically trained at the Juilliard School of Music, but as a young man he'd

A 1953 Comets holiday card featured Bill Haley, Marshall Lytle, Johnny Grande, Billy Williamson, and new drummer Charlie Higler (second from bottom).

found his true calling when he started sneaking uptown to Harlem's Shim Sham Club to hear the great black jazzman Eddie Dougherty pounding the skins in the house band. Eventually Gussak's flexibility and steady, almost perfect time made him an in-demand studio drummer.

When Dave Miller was ready to release "Real Rock Drive," the Saddlemen had already traded in their cowboy duds for suits, and all that remained now was to change their cowboy handle to something hipper, more dynamic. According to Haley, a program director at WPWA named Bob Johnson had suggested to him, "You know, with a name like yours you ought to call yourselves the Comets." He was referring to the similarity between Haley and Halley, the name of the British astronomer who in 1682 had first spotted and named Halley's Comet, which streaked past the earth every seventy-six years. Never mind that Sir Edmund Halley had pronounced his name something closer to Holly. To mid-twentieth-century Americans, it was *Haley's* Comet.

The group, including non-partner Marshall Lytle, agreed that the time had come to make their final break from country music. When "Real Rock Drive" came out in November 1952, the name on the label was Bill Haley With Haley's Comets. Bill Haley himself had not been born when Halley's Comet passed by in 1910, nor would he live to see it return in 1986, but that big chunk of icy rock would forever be linked to his name.

CHAPTER 6

CRAZY MAN, CRAZY

In late 1953 Bill Haley told the *Philadelphia Evening Bulletin* that after his high school assembly shows he would talk to the kids and jot down the expressions they used, like "man, that music's gone" and "dig that crazy rhythm," looking to find catchy phrases he could turn into songs. "I had a [studio] date to cut a record, and the day before the cutting, I hadn't decided what to play. I wanted to do something new, different. I had taken down a whole list of expressions I had heard kids use. Among them I had written 'crazy man.' The kids use crazy to mean anything exceptional, good. Like a necktie a boy's wearing. You say to him, 'That's crazy, man, crazy.'"

Marshall Lytle remembered the incident in more detail. "We did a [morning] show in Eddystone, just outside Chester, about a mile or two from where Bill lived at that time. Bill and I rode over together, and after the show, while we were loading instruments into the car, the kids gathered around, and Bill asked them how they liked our music. One kid said it was 'crazy, man, crazy!' So right after that, we went back to Bill's apartment where Bill's [second] wife, Cuppy [Joan Cupchak], was making lunch for us. Bill picked up his guitar and started singing 'crazy, man, crazy.' He and I wrote that song in thirty minutes. That's one of my sore spots, because I never got any credit for co-writing that song."

Dave Miller booked their "Crazy Man, Crazy" session at Coastal Studios in New York City. For the date, Haley brought back the two outside musicians who had played on "Real Rock Drive": drummer Billy Gussak and busy New York session guitarist Art Ryerson, a forty-year-old veteran of the Paul Whiteman

Orchestra who could play in any style. (Danny Cedrone was busy elsewhere with his own group's hit recording of Duke Ellington's "Caravan," which spent a week in the Top 30 in early 1953.) Gussak may have been the one who introduced Ryerson to Haley because they had worked together in Raymond Scott's orchestra for *Your Hit Parade*, a song-countdown TV show on NBC.

Like the repeating riff in "Real Rock Drive," the structure of "Crazy Man, Crazy" had been borrowed from Tennessee Ernie Ford's "Kissin' Bug Boogie," right down to Ryerson echoing the title's vocal hook on his six-string Gretsch. Otherwise, the song was *sui generis*. Gussak kicked it off with a *rat-a-tat* snare drum pattern interrupted by a trill from Ryerson—and the song was off and running. Ryerson dominated "Crazy Man, Crazy," quoting "Dixie" during his frantic solo and, near the end, repeating a wild lick like a honking saxophonist stuck on one note, accompanied by chaotic cheers of "Go! Go! Go! Go! Go!" from the band, as the song faded out.

Though recorded more than a year before what is now recognized as the rock 'n' roll era, the backbeat-heavy "Crazy Man, Crazy" was fully rock 'n' roll. It also set a standard for rock 'n' roll songs by recognizing that white kids were picking up black jazz slang left over from the twenties and thirties. Haley sang about finding a band with a "solid" beat, so that he could start "rockin'" with his "chick," 'cause "man, that music's gone, gone."

Though "crazy" had originally indicated mental impairment or mad obsession, by the early twentieth century objects or ideas could be crazy if they induced excitement or agitation. After Mamie Smith's "Crazy Blues," jazz-crazed Tin Pan Alley smithies were rhapsodizing about "Crazy Words—Crazy Tune" (1927), "Crazy Rhythm" (1928), and "Crazy Feet" (1930). "Chick"—a young, pretty girl who's hep to the jive—had been popular among Harlem musicians since the thirties. "Go," a term used since World War I for being in full swing, had resurfaced in jazz and R&B right after World War II, usually as a call from the crowd exhorting a frantic, overheated soloist to keep going. The logical extension of go was "gone," as in "real gone music," meaning it had reached beyond mundane reality. Though the Treniers, an energetic black combo, turned the chant into a frenzied R&B hit single called "Go! Go! Go!" as early as 1951, Haley claimed he picked it up elsewhere. "I remember watching a high school football game and the cheerleaders were saying, 'Go! Go! Go! Go! Go!' and the words came to me," he told deejay Roger Scott. "Go! Go! Go! Go! Everybody!" Haley recalled that when the Comets performed "Crazy Man, Crazy" live, the kids responded more to the "Go! Go!" chants than they

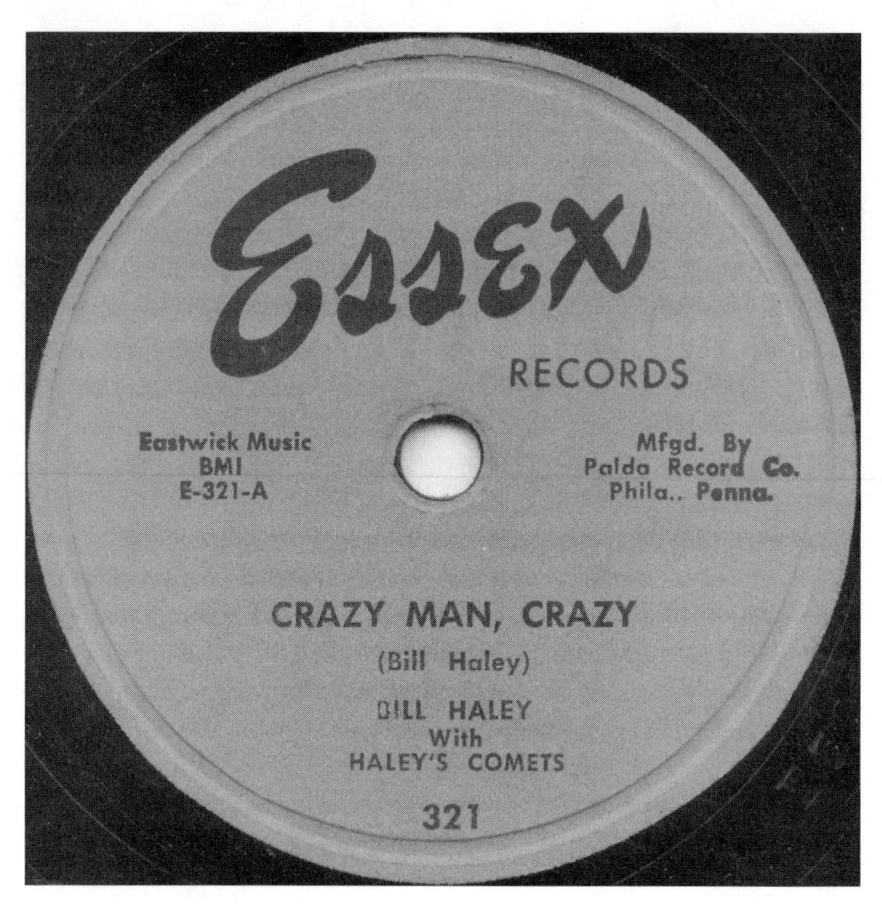

In 1953 "Crazy Man, Crazy" became the first pop hit—peaking at No. 12—that had what would later be called a distinct rock 'n' roll beat.

did to "crazy, man, crazy." "They marched almost as an army down the streets and all of them saying, 'Go! Go! Go! Go!'" It was like a mantra that bonded them together.

(Whether or not Haley got the chant from the Treniers, they had a strong influence on the Comets. Twins Claude and Cliff Trenier, after knocking around Los Angeles as vocalists in several bands, had put together a group similar to Louis Jordan's but featuring more acrobatic routines that included a honking, screeching alto saxophonist and a piano player who could do handstands on his keys as he kicked his feet in the air. By 1949 they were being billed as the Rockin' Rollin' Treniers. "I remember we were playing the Riptide in Wildwood, New Jersey [in 1953]," Claude Trenier told writer Nick Tosches.

"Bill Haley had a cowboy band that played right across the street from us [at the Hof Brau]. He used to come in and watch us. He asked us what we called the music we were playing. And we told him. Hell, we *told* him." Haley was so impressed that he gave them "Rock-a-Beatin' Boogie," the song he'd written for Danny Cedrone's Esquire Boys. The Treniers recorded it for Okeh Records in early 1954, a year and a half before Haley himself got around to cutting it.)

The release of "Crazy Man, Crazy" (the loss of the first comma was a printer's error on the label) came just as Essex Records was on a roll thanks to a freak novelty called "Oh Happy Day," written and recorded by a squeaky-voiced seventeen-year-old kid named Don Howard, that was currently No. 4 on the national charts. Distributors and disc jockeys were taking the new Essex releases more seriously now, and Dave Miller had more promotional money to throw around. His attention-grabbing trade paper ads screamed: "'Crazy Man, Crazy' is the new hot music for real cool cats!"

Small operations like Essex also had more access to radio stations in 1953 than ever before. Over the past several years, network radio dramas and comedies, from *The Adventures of Superman* to *The Adventures of Ozzie and Harriet*, had been migrating to the new medium of television, leaving behind vast stretches of empty airtime. "Radio is dead!" announced one TV network president, reasoning that since sound had put silent movies out of business in the late twenties, why wouldn't sound with pictures likewise doom mere aural programming? But there were still plenty of people who wanted to hear music over their radios, especially in their cars or at work. As disc jockeys rushed into the vacuum, record companies big and small were ready to support them with promotional records and ad revenue. Gradually it dawned on radio programmers that many of their listeners were teenagers wanting to get away from their parents in the TV den and groove to their own entertainment. According to the Record Industry Association of America, 1953 sales hit an all-time high of $205 million, up $16 million from 1952; most of that new activity was spurred directly by the explosion of radio disc jockeys.

The Comets were in the midst of a nine-week engagement at the Club Hof Brau in Wildwood, New Jersey, one of Philadelphia's oceanside playgrounds, when "Crazy Man, Crazy" broke wide open. In early May *Billboard* named it a "Best Buy" and *Cash Box* blessed it with "Sleeper of the Week." Haley later told the *Philadelphia Evening Bulletin*, "I knew I was on the right track because the kids began clapping in rhythm and yelling 'Go! Go! Go!' as they dug that beat. That's what we were selling…a beat the kids could dance to. It's the kids who buy the records today." On May 23, 1953, "Crazy Man, Crazy" entered *Billboard*'s Top 30 pop chart for what would be a ten-week run and reached as high as No. 12, at a time when a lush Percy Faith orchestral movie theme called "The Song From 'Moulin Rouge' (Where Is Your Heart)" was the nation's No 1 song for ten weeks in a row, having dislodged Patti Page's "(How Much Is) That Doggie in the Window." With Page, Perry Como, Teresa Brewer, and Eddie Fisher dominating the charts, "Crazy Man, Crazy" sounded very crazy indeed. The Ralph Marterie Orchestra gave the song a seal of approval by recording a cover version on Mercury Records featuring an R&B saxophonist. "Crazy Man, Crazy" was now such a centerpiece at Comets shows that Haley had to a hire a full-time drummer—twenty-nine-year-old Richard Boccelli, who worked under the name Dick Richards—to duplicate Billy Gussak's rapid-fire pyrotechnics.

"Crazy Man, Crazy" became so emblematic of disaffected youth that two months after falling off the charts it found its way into a national television production that touched upon juvenile delinquency. The ninety-minute program was *Glory in the Flower*, William Inge's first teleplay, airing live on CBS's *Omnibus* on Sunday, October 4, 1953. It starred a promising young actor, James Dean, as a rebellious kid named Bronco out on bail on a marijuana charge. Faced with ejection from a café for spiking his Coke from a pint of hooch in his jacket, he snarled at the owner, "I'm not gonna take orders from you. No one's gonna tell me what to do."

To set an insouciant and unpredictable mood, the producers of *Glory in the Flower* used "Crazy Man, Crazy" as a frame for the story. *Omnibus* host Alistair Cooke walked onto the café set to introduce the play, then dropped a coin into the jukebox to stir its actors into motion. The first person to hit the dance floor, swinging his shoulders and hips in a jitterbug, was James Dean; at the end of the program, "Crazy Man, Crazy" spun again as the scene faded to black.

The character of Bronco was a warm-up for Dean's sullen Jim Stark in the Warner Bros. film *Rebel Without a Cause* two years later, but Bronco was in fact the more dangerous rebel of the two. Stark may have been egged into a knife fight and a game of dragstrip chicken, but he was more alienated than damaged and more angry at his father's fecklessness than with society in general; unlike Bronco, Stark didn't take drugs and drink alcohol. He also wasn't listening to rock 'n' roll. The music coming through the radio in his Mercury sedan in *Rebel* was generic big band jazz, even though a disc jockey's voice at one point called it "rhythm and blues."

Dean would come to define the way a young white 1950s hipster sneered at convention as he languidly combed his hair, cocked his head, dangled his cigarette, turned up his jacket collar, and slunk into the seat of his hopped-up jalopy. In short, he personified the rebellious teenager turning away from his father's generation. In 1956 Dean became a posthumous rock 'n' roll icon—Elvis Presley's mythical fellow traveler. And yet, despite calling himself "a gone cat" on more than one occasion, he had no apparent affinity or connection to

James Dean (with Natalie Wood on the set of **Rebel Without a Cause***) first played a juvenile delinquent in a 1953 TV drama with a Bill Haley soundtrack.*

rock 'n' roll except for his love of LaVern Baker's mambo R&B hit, "Tweedlee Dee." Prone to slapping a set of bongos he often carried with him, Dean dug the bebop of Thelonious Monk and Charlie Parker, not Bill Haley or even Elvis, who was relatively unknown when Dean was killed in a September 30, 1955, car crash. In fact, since Dean was planning to drive on up to San Francisco later in the week of his death, he might have been hanging out with Jack Kerouac, Lawrence Ferlinghetti, and other bohemians on October 7, when Allen Ginsberg formally launched the beat revolution at the city's Six Gallery by reading his new bop prosody *Howl*. Only after Presley became a recording star, went to Hollywood in early 1956, surrounded himself with Dean's disciples, and pledged allegiance to the actor's ghost did James Dean become rock 'n' roll's patron saint. Part of it probably had to do with the fact that as a Method actor, Dean reached into his own emotional experiences to interpret the material he worked with, much the same way that R&B-inspired rock 'n' roll singers like Presley did. And yet his only real brush with rock 'n' roll—in *Glory in the Flower*, a title taken from poet William Wordsworth's line that "nothing can bring back the hour of splendor in the grass, of glory in the flower"—occurred, when Dean was still an unknown actor and rock 'n' roll music didn't yet have an identity. The only connection between the two was Bill Haley.

CHAPTER 7

PUT YOUR GLAD RAGS ON . . .

Ray Max Freedman was born in Philadelphia on January 8, 1893. As a young man with a quiet disposition and a facility for doggerel, he pursued a career as a song lyricist. Working with composer Harry D. Squires out of a small downtown office in the Lafayette Building, he churned out a number of Victorian ditties like "Her Beaus Were Only Rainbows," and a couple of them grabbed the ears of a major New York publisher, Joe Morris Music Company, which in 1918 placed "Some Day I'll Make You Glad" with silent film actress Ruth Roland, an early "queen of the westerns." Another actress, Donna Montran, who had a small part in D. W. Griffith's 1915 epic *Birth of a Nation*, recorded their next song, "In the Heart of a Fool." And, as pointed out in Chapter 2, the young men wrote "I've Got the Cryin' Blues" a year before Mamie Smith broke the blues barrier on wax. By now Freedman had dropped his first name and transformed himself into Max C. Freedman, perhaps because the girl he married was also named Ray (though she sometimes spelled it Rae). Like any levelheaded wife, Ray encouraged her husband to find a steady job, and as befit his unassuming personality he became a postal clerk, a position he would keep into old age regardless of the size of his royalty checks.

Though he managed to get a few songs published both as Max C. Freedman and Fred C. Mann (a name he used in the early 1940s, often to write lyrics for classical pieces such as Luigi Arditi's "Il Bacio"), none of them clicked until one day in late 1945, when he got together with a local radio personality named Dick Thomas (*né* Richard Thomas Goldhahn) to write a novelty tune under his

57

real name, Ray Freedman, called "Sioux City Sue"—whose best line was "your hair is red, your eyes are blue, I'd swap my horse and dog for you." Suddenly his twenty-five-year streak of so-so luck came to an end. Thomas's urban cowpoke soliloquy on National Records went to No. 1 on *Billboard*'s folk music (hillbilly) chart, spent a week in the Top 20, and inspired four hit cover versions, including Bing Crosby's No. 3 rendition in early 1946. Gene Autry recorded it as the centerpiece of his next movie, *Sioux City Sue*. The song turned out to be one of the better sellers that year and prompted Freedman to write a few more cowtown ballads like "The Beaut From Butte" and "I've Got a Gal in Laramie." But he wasn't able to come up with another hit until Morty Berk and Frank Capano asked him to help them with "Heartbreaker," the Ferko String Band hit, two years later. Eventually, Philadelphia being a small town as far as songwriters were concerned, he began working for music publisher Jimmy Myers.

James E. Myers was an extravert with the hale and hearty air of a buccaneer—a temperamental opposite of Max C. Freedman. He was born October 26, 1919, in Philadelphia, to a drummer father and a pianist mother. "I broke my father's bass drum when I was two," he said later, explaining his own musical direction. Growing up, he fell in love with the more drum-oriented big band

Max C. Freedman (right), using his real name Ray Freedman, wrote the 1945–46 hit, "Sioux City Sue," with radio cowboy Dick Thomas.

Max C. Freedman's professional songwriting career began in 1918 (above), thirty-five years before he wrote "Rock Around the Clock."

music of Tommy Dorsey and Benny Goodman. "When I was fourteen I started a group called Jimmy Myers & The Truckadeers Orchestra," he said. "We... worked fairly steady on the weekends. This was back when the 'trucking' dance was very popular." When trucking went out of style, he wanted a new name, both for himself and his band. "We went down to the phone company where they had walls of phone books from all over the United States. We pulled out books from Chicago, Detroit, Cleveland, Los Angeles, New York, and went through all of them. We couldn't find a Jimmy DeKnight—so we decided to call

CHAPTER 7: Put Your Glad Rags On . . . **59**

the band Jimmy DeKnight & His Knights of Rhythm." Myers learned the proprietary value of music after he picked a 1933 Bing Crosby song called "Blue Prelude" to be his band's theme. "Another bandleader came in one night and heard this song that we'd been using for about a year or two, and a few months later there's a [local] hit out by him called 'Blue Prelude.' That made me angry, so I decided to write a song of my own and copyright it. I wrote one called 'Things That You Say,' which we used for our theme song from then on."

Back home after serving in the South Pacific during World War II, Myers and an old friend, Jack Howard, dropped by the Pythian Temple on Broad Street in Philadelphia where a hillbilly radio show, *The Hayloft Hoedown*, aired every Saturday night on the ABC network. "[Jack] introduced me to all the country artists and talked me into starting Cowboy Records [with him]," Myers said, though no record exists of his co-owning Howard's Cowboy label. "We recorded people like Jesse Rogers, Shorty Long & The Santa Fe Rangers, Pee Wee Miller, and the entire *Hayloft Hoedown* crowd." The garrulous Myers had no trouble carrying a few 78s under his arm into the country music radio stations around Philadelphia and New York and getting someone to listen to them. "Everyone knew me, and when I walked in with a record, if it was decent, they would put it on the air." One of those disc jockeys was a one-eyed cat named Bill Haley at WPWA in Chester. As the two men became friendlier, Myers hired Haley's group to record some of his songs.

James Myers turned himself into an all-purpose enterprise. He convinced a Philadelphia businessman to hire him to promote three local country music bars. He formed an agency to book the acts that were recording on Cowboy Records, including the Saddlemen. And most crucially, he set up Myers Music and Jem Publishing (and later Standard Music) in order to own his artists' songs. By the early fifties one of Jem's hired guns was Max C. Freedman, who scribbled out a number of corny pop confections like "Tango of Lament" with a lady composer named Jean Carlo, and delivered various genres of song on demand, such as "Drunk as a Skunk" (with the Mallé brothers), "In Sun-Kissed Hawaii" (with John Nakula Kamano), "We'll Have a Red, White & Blue Christmas" (with Jesse Rogers), and "The Angels Were Singing Ave Maria" (with Frank Capano and Gaetano Pollizze). Freedman also shared a few writing credits with Myers's Jimmy DeKnight (sometimes alternately spelled De Knight) persona. In keeping with his backlog of western-flavored songs, one of his early collaborations with Myers was "The Covered Wagon Goes Roll, Roll, Rollin'."

Music publisher and promoter Jimmy Myers (with Bill Haley, above) was important to Haley's career, especially because he was responsible for Decca Records signing the Comets to a contract, but his role as a cowriter of "Rock Around the Clock" is questionable.

How they came up with "Rock Around the Clock" will probably never be fully sorted out. Freedman, who died in 1962, rarely spoke about it publicly, and Myers could never get his story straight during the countless times he regaled anyone who would listen. One account was that in 1953 Freedman brought him an incomplete tune titled either "Around the Clock" or "Dance Around the Clock," and that he (Myers) fine-tuned it into Bill Haley's best-known song. At other times Myers claimed he wrote the song himself and sought help from Freedman. "I had written the melody and about half of the lyrics, but I was having trouble with the rest of it. Max Freedman…walked into my office while I was fooling around with it one day and said, 'That sounds pretty good.

CHAPTER 7: Put Your Glad Rags On . . . **61**

Can I help you with it?' I said, 'Why not?' When we finished it, he said, 'What are you gonna call it?' I said, 'Rock Around the Clock.' And he said, 'Why rock, what's that mean? Why not "Dance Around the Clock"?' And I said, 'I just have a gut feeling, and since I'm half writer and whole publisher, I'm the boss.'" According to writer Chris Gardner, "When I met [Myers] in 1979, [he said] Max Freedman heard him playing the melody with one finger on the piano, came into the room and helped him to finish the song. He also says that he persuaded Freedman that 'Rock Around the Clock' was a better title than 'Dance Around the Clock.'" Myers told National Public Radio in 2000 that he wrote most of the words before Freedman ever saw the song. One name Myers certainly never mentioned was Sam Theard, author and singer of the earlier "Rock Around the Clock." The documentation that survives refutes most of Myers's self-aggrandizing lore. According to a songwriter's agreement between Freedman, Jimmy DeKnight, and Myers Music (witnessed by Jack Howard), dated October 23, 1952, a song called "(We're Gonna) Rock Around the Clock" was already in the works, months before Bill Haley wrote "Crazy Man, Crazy." Evidence suggests, however, that this contract was backdated a few months later in order to include Myers's participation. More certainly, we know that in early 1953 Freedman took the song, titled "We're Gonna Rock Around the Clock Tonight" (without any parentheses), to a local music copyist named Harry Filler, who transcribed it as a three-part arrangement. At the top of the handwritten music sheet, either Freedman or Filler jotted "words & music by Max C. Freedman." When the song was copyrighted (EP70269) with the U.S. Library of Congress on March 31, 1953, it bore the names Jimmy DeKnight and Max C. Freedman. The final title was "(We're Gonna) Rock Around the Clock."

So did Freedman write the song all by himself in his modest house at 1327 Spruce Street in Philadelphia? Where did Myers come in, and did he deserve half-composer credit? Over the last sixty-some years of Myers's life, the name of his DeKnight alter ego graced three hundred songs by his own count, yet only this one became a hit. Even after the astounding triumph of "Rock Around the Clock," he couldn't muster even a piddling follow-up. Perhaps the answer can be found in a $100,000 copyright infringement lawsuit that local music publisher Ivin Ballen of Gotham Music threatened to bring against Myers in late October 1955, accusing him of lifting "Rock Around the Clock" from "Rock the Joint." Myers's attorney, Edward D. Werblun, answered Ballen by stating for the record that the song "was written by Max Freedman, a freelance composer and songwriter, who sold the song to Myers." Werblun added

The original 1953 handwritten chart of "We're Gonna Rock Around the Clock Tonight!" was credited to Max C. Freedman, without Jimmy Myers.

that since Bill Haley had recorded both songs, "Naturally there would be some similarity between the two records." He mentioned nothing about Danny Cedrone's identical guitar solo on both performances, though it was most likely the source of Ballen's attention in the first place. The suit was quietly dropped, but the cat was out of the bag.

For anyone who can read music, a perusal of Freedman's original chart gives an insight into what may have first inspired the song. When he was learning his trade more than thirty years earlier, composers traditionally wrote an almost conversational verse that introduced the song but was melodically separate from it and not repeated once the chorus was underway. This was the case, for example, of Trixie Smith's original "My Man Rocks Me (With One Steady Roll)," with its opening blues lines. Or take Tin Pan Alley's idea of an around-the-clock song, Cole Porter's "Night and Day," with its famous intro that begins "Like the beat beat beat of the tom-toms." By the early 1950s these lyrical introductions were generally no longer used, but that didn't stop Max Freedman from beginning his song with an eight-bar instrumental verse whose minor-key changes sound like klezmer music—not surprising, given that he was the son of Jewish immigrants.

More notably, this verse has the distinctive syncopation of a 1951 hit recording on Decca Records by composer-conductor Leroy Anderson called "The Syncopated Clock." Anderson's gimmicky orchestral miniatures, such as "The Typewriter" and "Plink, Plank, Plunk," were wildly popular in the early 1950s, when fledgling TV stations needed pieces of incidental music to fill empty moments and hide technical gaffes. Everybody was familiar with the tunes even if they didn't know they had titles. But "The Syncopated Clock" was in a league of its own, drumming its insistent tick-tockery into tired minds every night for a dozen years after CBS began programming its wee hours with old Hollywood movies on *The Late Show*. That this monotonous ode to insomnia is most likely the rhythmic genesis of "Rock Around the Clock" is hilarious in its irony.

Myers claimed he first gave the song to Bill Haley when the Comets were in residency for a couple of months in Wildwood, New Jersey, during the early success of "Crazy Man, Crazy." Myers thought "Rock Around the Clock" would be a great follow-up, and Haley agreed. As the Comets began to work up the song onstage, it got a good reaction. "I had tried it out in the clubs, in the high schools, in the places I'd worked," Haley said later, "and everybody went crazy about the tune. I kept telling Dave [Miller], I said, 'Dave, this tune was written for me and I think every guy has one song and this is my tune.'"

But Miller refused to do any business with Myers because of some earlier deal gone sour. According to Haley, "Jimmy and Dave didn't like each other. Three times I took ['Rock Around the Clock'] into the recording studio and put it on the music rack, and every time Miller would see it, he'd come in and tear it up and throw it away. So I never could record it [for Essex]." As far as Miller was concerned, the Comets didn't need "Rock Around the Clock" because they already had several songs ready to go, including "Fractured," another jive novelty ("that music fractures me"). But despite its modest chart action in

August in the slipstream of "Crazy Man, Crazy," "Fractured" was forgettable and, worse, hard to dance to. Beyond the teenage slang in "Crazy Man, Crazy," Haley didn't seem to know what elements had made it so popular.

Most likely it was Myers who then passed the song along to a friend and fellow drummer, Paschal Vennitti, already a veteran of the Tommy Dorsey Orchestra despite his youthful age of twenty-four. He was born Adolph Leon Vennitti, but when Hitler shamed and discredited his christened name during the war, he changed it to Paschal to more befit his Italian-American background. But since Italian musicians generally played down their ethnicity with stage names, everybody knew him as Sonny Dae. In 1953 he was playing around the Philadelphia area with a combo called Sonny Dae and His Knights, whose name may have been a bow to Jimmy DeKnight and His Knights of Rhythm. Besides Vennitti, the group consisted of vocalist-pianist Hal Hogan, guitarist Art Buono, and a bassist whose name has been forgotten.

Myers's old Cowboy Records crony, Jack Howard, was now running a new company, Arcade Records, out of a Philadelphia music store, and if Essex wouldn't put the song out, Arcade would. So Myers, on his own dime, cut "Rock Around the Clock" with Sonny Dae and His Knights at the Reco Arts Studio on North Twelfth Street. Their greatest contribution to the song was changing Max Freedman's original tempo to a country shuffle, but otherwise they stayed faithful to the sheet music, right down to Freedman's not very lively key of F. "Rock Around the Clock" was Arcade's twenty-third single. Distribution probably didn't extend much beyond the Philadelphia area, and judging from the single's scarcity today, Jack Howard must have given up on it after a few weeks.

Meanwhile, Bill Haley was making the final important addition to the Comets' lineup that would complete their transformation from a country group doing rhythm and blues songs to a white R&B group: a saxophonist. At first Haley hired Anthony Liquori, professionally known as Tony Lance, to play baritone sax on a recording session that produced two songs. But the oversized baritone's bellow was too deep for a string band, and it was a hard instrument for a player to move around on with agility. Also, Lance wasn't a wailer like the era's top exhibitionist tenor men, known as "honkers." By the time the Comets returned to the studio near the end of 1953, Haley had opted for Joey D'Ambrosio, an eighteen-year-old Italian kid from North Philadelphia (born March 23, 1934) who could play like the R&B cats.

"In those days the only place you could work regularly were the bars, the

Sonny Dae and His Knights were (clockwise from left) singer-pianist Hal Hogan, drummer Paschal Vennitti, guitarist Art Buono, and an unidentified bass player.

strip clubs," said D'Ambrosio, who sometimes went by the name Joey Ambrose. "I'd walk the bar, walk through the audience, honking, playing 'Night Train.' I was influenced by the black musicians I'd seen down at Pep's Show Bar in Philly. It was a black place. My favorite honker was Red Prysock, who was with Tiny Bradshaw's band, but I learned a lot watching Lynn Hope and especially Big Jay McNeely when they were in town."

Though forgotten today, the honking tenor sax rage lasted from the mid forties until about 1953. Confined originally to Negro clubs, it crossed over, especially on the West Coast, around 1951, when white kids flocked to midnight shows where black horn players tried to upstage each other with acrobatics and manic shrieking. Some critics have likened honking—overplaying the saxophone and repeating one or two notes over and over—to the cadences of black Southern preachers who pounded relentlessly on the mantra-like sounds of words (Je-*sus*! Je-*sus*! Je-*sus*!), rather than use their meaning, in order to cut through the listener's intellect and go straight for the viscera; others said it was a venting of the frustration and anger that blacks felt after America reneged on its World War II promise of equality and returned to the same old racist system after the war ended. As writer Arnold Shaw put it, "In the monotonous honking and catlike screeching, [the honker] was mocking the audience and destroying the music." Poet Leroi Jones (now Amiri Baraka), in *Blues People*, agreed, claiming that black saxophonists were making "the instrument sound as unmusical, or as non-Western, as possible."

The general public got its first taste of the honking technique on Lionel Hampton's 1943 hit Decca version of "Flying Home," featuring a young Texas tenorist named Illinois Jacquet. Then, in July 1944, at the first Jazz at the Philharmonic concert in Los Angeles, Jacquet went full tilt, blasting a five-minute temper tantrum that drove the audience into near hysteria. Before long, the "sepia" charts were full of tenor players, young and old, bleating and squealing on instrumentals like "Cornbread" (Hal Singer) and "We're Gonna Rock" (Wild Bill Moore). They often had colorful names like Gatortail Jackson, Floorshow Culley, Long Gone Chamblee, Lockjaw Davis, and Blowtop Lynn, usually taken from their most popular song titles. Leroi Jones, in a 1967 remembrance called "The Screamers," recounted seeing Lynn Hope, an early convert to the Nation of Islam who began wearing a turban onstage around 1950, performing at a Newark club. Walking atop the bar and weaving through the audience, Hope began hitting on "one scary note" over and over again, driving the crowd of five hundred "hopped-up woogies" into such a frenzy that they followed Hope like mice behind the Pied Piper. "Ecstatic, completed, involved in a secret communal experience," they trailed Hope out onto Belmont Street, "laughing at the dazed white men who sat behind the wheels." When riot police arrived to break up the party, Hope and his followers returned triumphantly to the club, all screaming in unison that "scary note." Jones called the agonized honking an amplification of "the Black scream."

By 1951, several Los Angeles saxophonists, including Big Jay McNeely and Joe Houston, were packing late-night movie houses and auditoriums with mostly white and Chicano teenagers. Wearing neon-colored suits, McNeely squirmed on his back with his feet kicking in the air, or walked through the crowd and sometimes out the door, playing in the street to the accompaniment of honking motorists. At one point he was arrested on a San Diego sidewalk for disturbing the peace. In San Francisco he left a club and hopped on a cable car, with half of the patrons and part of his band trailing behind him. *Life* magazine ran photos of him thrashing onstage, blowing his horn toward the ceiling while hundreds of kids grooved to the cacophony with dazzled eyes.

This note-thumping, repetitive honking, according to one publication, made listeners twitch around "like Watusis." White parents became alarmed that their blissed-out children were under the influence of black shamans; a panel of psychiatrists reportedly showed up at a McNeely concert to observe the hysteria; finally, Los Angeles city officials stepped in, invoking fire and health codes to close down the shows, forcing McNeely and the others to take their act on the road, where their energies were largely dissipated.

Joey D'Ambrosio had begun imitating the honkers to rouse the crowds at his own Friday night gig at a teenage club. "The owner of the place knew Bill Haley, and he knew that Bill was looking for a saxophone player.... So he set me up with Dave Miller and I auditioned for the band at [road drummer] Dick Richards's house and Bill hired me on a try-out basis.... Bill wasn't sure if he wanted to add me on a permanent basis until we did a teenage dance in Baltimore and I went into the audience during my solo. The kids really loved it, they went wild.... Bill had never seen that kind of reaction before, and that locked up the job for me. Bill told me I was now a full-time Comet."

In early 1954, Jimmy Myers contacted several A&R men from the major record companies about the possibility of signing Bill Haley and His Comets away from Essex Records. Steve Sholes at RCA Victor and Mitch Miller at Columbia expressed only mild interest, but Decca Records' Milt Gabler was enthusiastic. "Myers called from Philadelphia, made an appointment, and asked if I knew Bill," Gabler recalled. "I said, 'Of course. I remember "Crazy Man, Crazy."' He said, 'Well, he's available.' I said, 'Well, come on up and I'll talk to you about it.'" Thanks to his longtime association with Louis Jordan and His Tympany Five, Gabler was the one major record executive who could appreciate what the Comets could do.

Decca had been the most adventurous of the big labels since Jack Kapp founded it in 1934, braced with startup capital and any catalog selections he needed from the British Decca Recording Company. While other majors jettisoned Negro artists during and after the Depression, Decca made a point of keeping them onboard, especially the Mills Brothers, the Ink Spots, Lucky Millinder, Lionel Hampton, Jimmie Lunceford, Ella Fitzgerald, and Louis Jordan. In fact, Kapp hired Gabler in 1941 precisely for his jazz background and his familiarity with black music in general.

Born May 20, 1911, to Jewish immigrant parents in New York City, Gabler learned the music business out of his father's Commodore Music Shop on East 42nd Street, Manhattan's premier jazz store where the local hipsters and musicians hung out. In the 1930s he set up his own label, Commodore Records, to record his friends, who included Lester Young, Louis Armstrong, and Billie Holiday. With Holiday he cut "Strange Fruit," a now-famous indictment of Southern lynching, written by a white New York poet, that her previous label, Columbia, had refused to record.

Among his first duties at Decca was producing Louis Jordan, who had already been with the label for a couple of years without much success. Jordan was an accomplished alto saxophonist and blues vocalist who could entertain any audience, black or white. He may not have been the first one to strip the traditional big band down to five or six guys who could swing better, but he was the first who made it a formula for hit records. During World War II, Jordan and His Tympany Five were so popular with servicemen that two of his records went to No. 1 on *Billboard*'s national country music chart, including "Is You Is or Is You Ain't (Ma' Baby)"; its flipside, "G.I. Jive," was No. 1 on both the sepia and pop charts—which means that the single itself (both sides together) topped all three main charts, a feat duplicated only once, a dozen years later, with Elvis Presley's "Hound Dog"/"Don't Be Cruel." In all, under Gabler's production ear, eighteen of Louis Jordan's singles were No. 1 sepia hits between 1942 and 1950, and several of them, such as "Choo Choo Ch' Boogie" and "Ain't Nobody Here but Us Chickens" (the flipside of Sam Theard's "Let the Good Times Roll"), lingered at the top for several months. Over a dozen of them also crossed over into pop music's Top 20. More than any other artist, Louis Jordan, with his shuffle rhythms, riffing horns, stinging blues guitarists, and perpetual good humor, established the parameters of what became rhythm and blues in the last half of the 1940s.

But by 1953 Jordan was fifty-five years old and hadn't had a hit for a couple of years. His emerging diabetes kept him from going on the extended tours that had been so necessary to his success, and his happy-go-lucky, self-deprecating music didn't interest younger blacks, who preferred hard-edged urban blues or bebop jazz. The white kids listening to R&B for the first time couldn't relate to him, either. Decca quietly allowed Jordan's contract to expire at the beginning of 1954, leaving Gabler with a vacancy in his roster.

As Jordan himself said in the 1970s, "When Bill Haley came along in '53 he was doing the same shuffle boogie I was. Only he was goin' faster than I was."

Around that same time, Milt Gabler told Arnold Shaw, "We'd begin [at the Comets' sessions] with Jordan's shuffle rhythm. You know, dotted eighth notes and sixteenths, and we'd build on it. I'd sing Jordan riffs to the group that would be picked up by the electric guitars and tenor sax.... They got a sound that had the drive of the Tympany Five and the color of country and western."

But this is getting ahead of the story, because Bill Haley and His Comets were still under contract to Dave Miller's company, and even though it was due to expire on April 8, Miller had the option of renewing it for another year as long as he notified Haley or his manager in writing "at least 30 days prior to the expiration," *i.e.*, on or before March 8. Why wouldn't he want to re-sign his most popular recording act, especially if he knew a major record company was interested? Gabler was willing to offer a buy-out, but Myers informed him that Miller was presently in West Germany recording an orchestra for his new budget-line classical label, blissfully diverted and unaware that time and Bill Haley were about to slip away from him. When March 8 passed, the Comets were legally free to sign with Decca as soon as the contract ended.

Myers and Haley drove to New York on April 1 and met with Gabler in his office to discuss the terms of their new one-year deal. Decca would release four singles, pay a five-percent royalty against a $5,000 advance, and give each record full publicity support, including two thousand deejay copies sent to stations around the country and major ads placed in *Billboard* and *Cash Box*. As Myers's consideration for setting up the deal, he would pick the B-side songs for all four singles from his own publishing company. The first one, naturally, would be "Rock Around the Clock," a throwaway as far as Milt Gabler was concerned.

CHAPTER 8

ROCKIN' UP IN SEVENTH HEAVEN

The Comets' first session for Decca Records was scheduled for Monday morning, April 12, 1954, at eleven o'clock, at the company's Studio A, located in Manhattan on the first floor of the Pythian Temple at 135 West 70th Street, between Broadway and Columbus. Built in 1927 as a headquarters and meeting place for a national fraternal organization called the Knights of Pythias, the eleven-story building was an extraordinary Egyptian-deco homage to King Tut on an otherwise nondescript side street of brownstones and office buildings. Inside, Decca's studio, formerly a ballroom, had a stage large enough to accommodate an orchestra. Marshall Lytle remembers it as "like a legitimate theater with a stage and a nice sound in it." Milt Gabler liked the place because he could arrange his artists onstage and capture their live-on-Saturday-night performances, enhanced by the natural echo from the room's high ceiling and walnut-paneled walls. To fully capture its acoustical warmth, Decca had recently installed a high-fidelity soundboard and a state-of-the-art mono Ampex tape recording machine.

As Gabler, Jimmy Myers, head engineer Larry McIntire, and the session drummer, Billy Gussak, waited well past eleven o'clock, there was no sign of Bill Haley and His Comets. "Where in the hell are they?" Gabler grumbled, pacing the floor as he puffed on one of Myers's Havana cigars. "Don't they have telephones in Chester?" Gabler had scheduled a double session—six hours—because the band had to learn one of the songs from scratch, and already the first hour was almost gone.

71

By noon Gabler was apoplectic. "Why didn't the bastards at least call?" he shouted at Myers. Before Myers could apologize, a secretary from Decca's corporate offices on West 37th Street called to tell them the Comets had been waylaid. The Chester-Bridgeport ferry had run aground on a sand bar midway across the Delaware River, stranding the group until a tugboat arrived to pull the ferry into deeper water. But the boys had already landed on the New Jersey side, the secretary said, and they'd be in New York—a hundred-mile drive, give or take—by one o'clock. Jimmy Myers suggested that they break for lunch—no sense in sitting around watching the clock and getting even more frustrated. Gabler, a roly-poly man with an obvious fondness for food, seconded the idea. "Call us when they get here," he told McIntire. He led Myers and Gussak out onto the noisy street and around the corner to a favorite deli on Broadway.

When they returned to the studio around one, Bill Haley's cream-colored 1954 Cadillac Seville was parked out front. The long hood was still hot enough to make the air shimmer as the musicians unpacked their instruments, joking about their death-defying dash into the city with Madman Haley at the wheel. Haley himself apologized to Gabler and thanked him for holding the session open. But the producer was having second thoughts. There were still four hours on the clock, but the band hadn't set up, hadn't learned the song he had picked for them to record, hadn't even seen it yet.

"Don't worry, Mr. Gabler," Haley assured him. "We've already got our song down pat, and it won't take us long to run down yours."

Gabler reflexively checked his watch. "All right, let's hurry it up. But next time we have a recording date, take the bridge."

The Comets set up their equipment on the stage as Larry McIntire and his assistant adjusted their microphones. Since the guys hadn't eaten, Lord Jim Ferguson ran out to get sandwiches. "All right, I want you down here facing the guys," Gabler told Haley, gesturing at a spot below the stage where a microphone and a music stand were set up next to each other on the polished wooden floor.

Haley thought it was odd, him standing four feet below his own band, looking up at them like a New York tourist. After all the years of huddling together around one or two microphones in radio stations and crackerbox studios, this seemed like an impersonal and fragmented way of making a record. Also, the acoustics on the stage, with its lower, separate ceiling, were different from down where he was standing. He figured, well, this is the way the big boys do things.

At Decca's Studio A at the Pythian Temple, producer Milt Gabler stands below the stage, giving directions to the Comets at a later session, probably in 1956.

Gabler gave the sheet music for "Thirteen Women (And Only One Man in Town)," the song slated to be the hit side of the Comets' first Decca single, to Johnny Grande, the only Comet besides Joey D'Ambrosio who could read music. Grande ran it down on the studio piano for the other musicians, and as they tentatively learned the chord changes and began to work out an arrangement, with a few added suggestions from Gabler, the engineer fine-tuned the sound he was getting through the board and occasionally sent his assistant out to move a microphone. As Gabler later told writer Jas Obrecht, "It took them a while to learn their riffs and get their notes, but when it was all done, you could get two or three great takes."

Bill Haley was skeptical about "Thirteen Women." The lyric sheet was on his music stand for one reason: Gabler contractually had the choice of what the A-side of every Comets single would be. What Haley didn't know was that Gabler also had a proprietary interest in "Thirteen Women." More important, Haley could see from the outset that the bizarre novelty tune would require some magic from the band to make it work. It was also in F, one of the darker keys. Haley preferred the more exuberant A or C, but Gabler insisted on keeping the song in F to match its downbeat subject.

Gabler's belief that the band could do justice to "Thirteen Women" was based on his underlying premise for signing them in the first place: that Bill Haley and His Comets were the natural heirs of Louis Jordan and His Tympany Five. Jordan had made his fortune recording goofy, offbeat material like "Thirteen Women" for Gabler, so why couldn't Haley do the same?

Originally titled "Thirteen Women And One Man," the song had been written and recorded by a black jazz guitarist named Dickie Thompson. Born in Jersey City, New Jersey, in 1917, Thompson had picked up a guitar in his early teens, flipped it upside down (rather than restringing it) to accommodate his dominant left hand, and taught himself to play sufficiently well by the time he left high school that he got steady work in shake-dance joints and other black

Dickie Thompson's original rhythm and blues version of "Thirteen Women and One Man" ran into censorship problems in early 1954.

clubs around his home town. In the early forties Thompson fell into New York City's jazz scene as a note-bending, bebop version of Django Reinhardt. He worked with drummer Cozy Cole, tenor saxophonist Clifford Scott (who would go on to co-write "Honky Tonk" in the mid fifties), and singer Dinah Washington. In 1946 he made a record under his own name—Dickie Thompson & His Blue Five—for the Signature jazz label. Five years later, Milt Gabler hired him for a brief Decca stint to cover Johnnie Ray's first single, "Whiskey and Gin."

In 1953, when Thompson signed with song publisher Danby Music to make demo records for other songwriters, the gig enticed him to try his own hand at composing. One day while he was moving into a new house and cleaning out an old shed in back, he found a soiled, beat-up copy of a 1931 potboiler by Tiffany Thayer called *Thirteen Women*. He didn't recognize the once-best-selling author, nor did he have any idea that RKO Pictures had turned the novel about a murderous ex-sorority Eurasian girl into a strange 1932 police procedural film whose claim to fame was that it featured the only credited onscreen appearance of Peg Entwistle, a British actress who became so distraught after her role was trimmed in the editing room that she famously jumped to her death off the top of the fifty-foot-high H of the Hollywoodland (now Hollywood) sign. Dickie Thompson tossed the book away, but the title intrigued him.

"I just sat down and wrote a song about me and thirteen women," Thompson said recently. "We cut it in the studio and Mickey Baker played guitar. It was [Danby] who set it up with the record company"—an indie label, Herald Records. Thompson sang in the dramatic baritone style of black pop singer Roy Hamilton, while the drummer rapped out a steady cha-cha rhythm.

> "Well, there was a-thirteen women and only one man in town
> There was a-thirteen women and only one man in town
> And funny as it may be, the one and only man in town was me
> With thirteen women and only one man in town.
> ….
>
> Well, let me tell you that I was the only man alive
> They sure kept me feeling good.
> Lord knows I was living, but just how long could I last?
> Then I decided to say goodbye, 'cause these girls were driving me mad
> Thirteen women and only one man in town."

Herald Records released "Thirteen Women and One Man" in early March

1954. The timing seemed right because the company was sizzling on the R&B circuit with a string of hits by churchy songbird Faye Adams and a vocal group called the Embers. With Herald's twenty distributors around the country ready to promote the record, it got airplay in several key cities. But suddenly, within a week or two, the single ran into trouble. Even for an R&B song "Thirteen Women and One Man" was more suggestive than many disc jockeys, advertisers, and station bosses felt comfortable with. One verse—"Two girls to give me my money, two girls to buy my clothes, and another sweet thing bought me a diamond ring, about forty carats, I suppose"—blatantly described a pimp's relationship with his whores, and other lines—"just like a fool I tried to love

Singer-guitarist Dickie Thompson wrote "Thirteen Women and One Man" without the nuclear theme of Bill Haley and His Comets' cover version.

'em all" and "I had thirteen beautiful women givin' everything they could"—sounded orgiastic.

Cash Box ran the following item: "New York, April 3—Dickie Thompson's Herald disk of 'Thirteen Women and One Man' has been banned on station WHOM in New York. Nevertheless, WHOM platter spinner Ray Carroll is doing his bit for the record by spinning the flip side ['I'm Innocent'] and describing the contents of 'Thirteen Women' and playing it as far as it is permissible. Disk is reportedly getting a definite reaction in Pittsburgh, Cincinnati, Cleveland, Atlanta and New Orleans." Radio resistance wasn't necessarily fatal. The Midnighters' "Work With Me, Annie," released less than a month earlier, was toiling its way toward the top of the R&B charts despite being censored from the airwaves. But "Thirteen Women and One Man" was not a strong enough recording to make up the difference on ghetto jukeboxes and word of mouth. Herald stopped promoting Thompson's single and left it dead in its tracks. "All of a sudden nobody was playing it anymore," he said.

Milt Gabler, who had used Louis Jordan to cover dozens of indie R&B recordings, thought that if the song were refined, it would be perfect for his new charge, Bill Haley, and more appropriate for a mainstream audience. He promptly contacted Danby Music and reportedly cut a deal that guaranteed a new Decca recording of "Thirteen Women and One Man" if Danby would pay Gabler a thousand dollars to rewrite it. "I didn't want any censor with the radio to bar the record from being played," Gabler told John Swenson. As Thompson recalled with a tinge of bitterness, "Gabler got paid outright for the first verse. All he wrote were the opening lines, 'Last night I was dreamin', dreamed about the H-bomb....'"

Actually Gabler, besides changing the song's awkward title to the more mellifluous "Thirteen Women (And Only One Man in Town)," had significantly changed a priapic fantasy into a post-apocalyptic idyll. Little more than a year had passed since the United States upped the Cold War ante by detonating the first hydrogen bomb in late 1952, ushering in a new generation of thermonuclear weaponry capable of destroying civilization. So naturally the H-bomb—"The Bomb"—was on everyone's mind. One rhythm and blues singer was already making records under the name H-Bomb Ferguson. And though plenty of songs had been recorded about the power or the implications of the earlier atomic bomb (such as hillbilly singer Lowell Blanchard's "Jesus Hits Like an Atomic Bomb" and the Golden Gate Quartet's "Atom and Evil"), the retooled "Thirteen Women" was the first recording about anyone surviving a nuclear holocaust—and enjoying the aftermath. With its tongue-in-cheek insouciance, the song mirrored the words of Chicago publisher Hugh Hefner, who six months earlier had introduced the inaugural issue of his *Playboy* magazine by saying, "If we are able to give the American male a few extra laughs and a little diversion from the anxieties of the Atomic Age, we'll feel we've justified our existence."

As Gabler went over the song with the Comets in the studio, they made several further revisions. Thompson had written "Thirteen Women" in a chord sequence of F-minor/C-sharp/C-sharp minor that sounded discordant to the average listener's ear, so Billy Williamson created a distraction by zinging eerie steel-guitar glissandos—called glisses among musicians—that seemed to spiral into the atmosphere. To make the song more danceable, Gabler suggested that the rhythm section underpin it with a rumba-flavored bass line packaged in a musical figure taken directly from Clyde McPhatter & The Drifters' "Such a Night," which on April 12, 1954, was riding near the top of the R&B charts. This particular four-note riff was a slight variant of a three-note bass line (harmonically the root, third, and fifth of the chord), pioneered by R&B producer Jesse Stone, that had become almost standard on black recordings by 1954, and which by 1956 would be rock 'n' roll's primary signature on songs like "Don't Be Cruel." Marshall Lytle on bass, Johnny Grande on piano, Danny Cedrone on electric guitar, and Joey D'Ambrosio on sax took only a couple of run-throughs to lock into this repeating figure so tightly they sounded like an orchestra.

When the tape finally began to roll, the band went directly into the four-note Drifters riff, and Haley sang:

> "Last night I was dreamin', dreamed about the H-bomb
> Well, the bomb went off and I was caught
> I was the only man on the ground.
> There was thirteen women and only one man in town...."

In describing the setup, Milt Gabler had added a sense of innocent fun.

> "I had two gals every mornin'
> Seein' that I was well fed
> And believe you me, one sweetened my tea
> While another one buttered my bread."

But then Haley returned to the original song, hinting at a more intimate arrangement with the girls:

> "Two gals gave me my money

>Two gals made me my clothes
>And another sweet thing bought me a diamond ring
>About 40 carats, I suppose.
>Well, thirteen women and only one man in town
>There was a-thirteen women and only one man in town...."

At the end of these last two lines Billy Williamson added a few leering licks on his steel guitar, like nudges in the listener's ribs.

>"It was something I can't forget
>And I think of those thirteen women yet
>It was thirteen women and me the only man in town."

At the end of the chorus, Danny Cedrone slipped into an ominous solo, complete with a dissonant flatted-fifth note, that on one level elaborated on the melody, albeit in a minor key, of another ode to sexual possessiveness: the 1942 Glenn Miller hit, "Don't Sit Under the Apple Tree (With Anyone Else but Me)." It also happened to be the melody of an old, apocalyptic spiritual, "Joshua Fit the Battle of Jericho," with its unspoken hook line: "and the walls came a-tumblin' down." Whether Cedrone made these connections consciously is anyone's guess.

>"I had three gals dancin' a mambo...."

At this point, Johnny Grande, who had been so integrated into the rhythm ensemble that his piano had been indistinguishable, suddenly leapt out to finger a quick mambo line, then just as quickly disappeared again for the rest of the recording.

>"...Three gals ballin' the jack
>And all of the rest really did their best
>Boy, they sure were a lively pack."

For the finale Bill Haley brought the song back to earth and, like Dickie Thompson before him, reassured the listener that all was well: "I woke up and I ended the dream, 'cause I had to get to work on time."

With the clock ticking and Jimmy Myers more jittery by the moment, the Comets recorded six takes of "Thirteen Women" and listened to all six playbacks before Gabler was satisfied. Though the Comets' arrangement was miles ahead of the original and more elaborate than anything they had previously done, Gabler realized that he was not going to get a comedic performance out of Bill Haley. Louis Jordan would have goggled his eyes and made "Thirteen Women" mildly amusing without breaking a sweat, but Haley lacked Jordan's impish humor. So in the end, "Thirteen Women" turned out to be as funny as, well, a mushroom cloud. But with its strange chords and eerie glisses, at least it sounded like no other record on the market.

When Gabler finally announced that he had a master take he could live with, only forty minutes remained. Glancing up at the studio clock on the wall, he said, "I hope you guys don't need any rehearsal time with the clock song. We've only got time for a couple of takes."

The Comets looked at each other. They had been road-testing "Rock Around the Clock" in clubs for months, and making a few final adjustments had been a piece of cake during rehearsal last night in Haley's basement, but now they were tired and burned out from "Thirteen Women." Also, two of the musicians were unfamiliar with the song. Billy Gussak was working full-time now in New York City as a studio drummer on NBC-TV's *Your Hit Parade*—a weekly rehashing of the nation's top hits. Dick Richards, the Comets' road drummer, briefly coached Gussak on where Haley wanted the snare drum to enhance the arrangement, but otherwise he was winging it. Also, since Art Ryerson, Haley's regular studio guitarist during the previous year, was now working with Mitch Miller across town at Columbia Records, Haley had called Danny Cedrone at the last minute, even though he hadn't sat in with the Comets since their "Rockin' Chair on the Moon" session in mid-1952. Serendipitously, the two men's unfamiliarity with "Rock Around the Clock" would give the recording some of its most dazzling moments, but nobody knew that at the time.

At last, as the clock reached four-thirty, with a half hour left in the session, the engineer announced, "'Rock Around the Clock,' take one. One, two...."

Gussak rapped a double rim shot loaded with echo and Bill Haley called out a one-note chant: "One, two, three o'clock, four o'clock *rock*...." Two more rim shots cracked through the mikes, as Haley modulated up a third of an octave to C-sharp: "Five, six, seven o'clock, eight o'clock *rock*...." Then rising again to E: "Nine, ten, eleven o'clock, twelve o'clock rock, we're gonna *rock* [the rhythm section hits a solid chord] *around* [another chord] the clock tonight...."

Joey D'Ambrosio recalled, "The beginning—the 'one, two, three o'clock, four o'clock *rock*'—was Dick Richards' idea. It worked right away. The song just happened. We hit a groove." Actually, counting up the clock came from Max C. Freedman's original sheet music and had been repeated in the Sonny Dae recording. This four-bar intro is what British musicologist Ian Whitcomb calls a "ready-steady-go," which translates in American English to ready-set-go. "It's a device from the nineteenth-century German marches," says Whitcomb. "There would be a couple of bars of music, separate from the song itself but attached to it all the same, that announced to the dancers that the next dance was beginning, and its tempo would tell them what dance step they'd be doing. It was a convention of the Victorian ballroom. For example, every Scott Joplin rag had a ready-steady-go." Furthermore, the imagery of "Rock Around the Clock" lent itself to having the vocalist take a quick clockwise spin from one to twelve before getting to the body of the song. For an entertainer like Bill Haley, whose music had always lived and breathed in dance halls where he not only sang but often "called" square dances, this introduction was standard fare.

What Dick Richards had actually suggested was a dynamic restructuring of the way this ready-set-go was delivered. Whereas on the earlier Arcade single Sonny Dae and His Knights had used a variation of Freedman's original eight-bar instrumental opening verse, the Comets dropped it altogether and went straight into the intro itself. And the Knights' lead vocalist, Hal Hogan, singing as part of an ensemble, had simply rattled off the numbers, staying on the same note (F-minor) until they reached "eight o'clock rock" (F-major). And when they chanted "we're gonna rock a-round the clock tonight" with a

Milt Gabler (right) goes over an arrangement with Bill Haley in Studio A. Haley's manager, Lord Jim Ferguson (glasses) stands ready to give valuable advice.

metronomic cadence, it lacked conviction. They sounded as if they'd be lucky to make it past nine o'clock. Nothing was dramatically emphasized—there was no "eight o'clock *rock*." Sonny Dae and his group had simply recorded the song as a loose shuffle, with a tick-tock boogie swing, in a pale imitation of any number of Louis Jordan songs.

The Comets vastly improved "Rock Around the Clock" by moving it out of F—essentially a piano key—and into A, a brighter guitar key. And by opening the song with an A-major triad—from bottom to top, A, C-sharp, and E—they outlined the song's three notes and cued the listener that it was a blues with no harmonic surprises. The real innovation, it turned out, was the drumming of Billy Gussak, who changed the song's rhythmic emphasis from moment to moment by accenting different beats—sometimes both the second and fourth, other times only the fourth—on the snare drum and cymbals, maintaining constant shifts in the drive of the performance.

"Put your glad rags on and join me, hon
We'll have fun till the clock strikes one...."

Already Bill Haley was making a melodic change. The verses on the Sonny Dae record were ascending second notes, but Haley stepped up to every third note. More specifically, he scrapped the melody of Freedman's verse and dropped in, almost note for note, the verse from one of his favorite records, Hank Williams's 1949 hit, "Move It On Over," which Williams in turn had partially recycled from an old, common New Orleans Mardi Gras riff; boogie-woogie pianist Little Brother Montgomery used it on his 1930 recording of "Vicksburg Blues," and a dozen years later bandleader Charlie Barnet made it the main hook of a popular instrumental called "Victory Walk." Like so much of "Rock Around the Clock," the verse was simply scraps of American music patched together.

"... We're gonna rock around the clock tonight
We're gonna rock rock rock till broad daylight
We're gonna rock, gonna rock around the clock tonight."

Haley also made another important change early in the song. Since Freedman had not written an eight-bar bridge linking the chorus to the verse—a staple of Tin Pan Alley songs, but nonexistent in the early blues tradition—the recording of "Rock Around the Clock" needed something extra to break up the repetition, namely a guitar solo. On Sonny Dae's recording, guitarist Art Buono hadn't slipped in until after the third chorus (following the "we'll be rockin' up in seventh heaven" verse), a minute and ten seconds into the recording; he had opened his solo with a drowsy quote from the nursery rhyme "rock-a-bye baby in the tree top," then meandered off into a sixteen-bar, bass-string lullaby. But Bill Haley, hoping to keep his audience awake and rocking, tapped Danny Cedrone to jump in right after the second chorus—only forty seconds into the recording—to give the song a jolt. Cedrone, playing his electrified Gibson ES-300, didn't disappoint. Earning every cent of the $41.25 that Haley was paying him for the session, he blazed into the same astonishing run—note for note—that he'd played two years earlier on "Rock the Joint," ended the solo by rippling down the scale, then fell in with Marshall Lytle's walking bass pattern to usher Haley back into the song.

According to Lytle, "Bill always wanted a guitar solo on his recordings, so Danny Cedrone was fooling around, trying to create a solo, and we were so short on time that I told Danny to do his solo from 'Rock the Joint.'" Joey D'Ambrosio concurred. "Marshall is the one that suggested that Danny play the solo from 'Rock the Joint.' It fit so well, and I said, 'No one ever heard "Rock the Joint" anyway.' It was in the same key and everything." Though Cedrone's bulky, honey-brown Gibson was not an easy instrument to control, he played with such dexterity and virtuosity that Haley's later guitarists would confess they were unable to duplicate the performance.

What we now think of as a "guitar solo"—a band's guitarist going off on his own instead of repeating the song's melody—harkens back to the late 1920s. Orchestra guitarists usually played banjos in the studio before 1925, because the old conical horn—the acoustic ear—couldn't hear the guitar very well above the other instruments. But with the introduction of the more sensitive electric microphone, followed by the Gibson Company's new steel-stringed L-5 model, guitarists like Nick Lucas, an easygoing Italian-American recording star, could make pop hits that showcased the instrument's warm tones. By 1927, jazz guitarists like Eddie Lang (recording with Bix Beiderbecke's band) and Lonnie Johnson (with Louis Armstrong's Hot Five) began stretching out and wandering away from the melodies when they soloed. But perhaps the first full-blown flight of improvisational fancy occurred in 1933, when Teddy Bunn, who played guitar with the Spirits of Rhythm, a black vocal group, soared through a 64-bar peregrination on "I've Got the World on a String" that remains breathtaking even today.

As Haley sang the next two choruses, the Comets drove the beat with stabbing chords that increasingly foreshadowed what was coming: the second instrumental break, in which the entire band vamped on a succession of stac-

Three months before his tragic death, Danny Cedrone laid down rock 'n' roll's first acclaimed guitar solo in Bill Haley's "Rock Around the Clock."

cato notes. This was basically a classic tenor sax break, but D'Ambrosio's honking was reinforced by the band's guitars—Williamson's steel, Cedrone's electric, and Haley's acoustic—and Johnny Grande's piano.

D'Ambrosio claimed they had worked out this basic arrangement at the rehearsal the night before. "The reason I came up with my honking part," he said, "was that the song was in the key of A, which put [my sax] in the key of B, and I could barely play in that key. So when they said, 'Joey, you take a solo at this point,' I made it easy for myself by playing one note." But during the rehearsal it had become obvious that the song was building to such a crescendo that it needed more than just one instrument. "I thought we'd get more excitement out of it by doing something the whole band could join in on. That's what rhythm and blues combos would often do." Underlying all this rhythm was Marshall Lytle's percussive performance on his standup bass, slapping his hand against the fingerboard, then plucking the strings as he jerked his hand away, creating a steady *"ka-chunk-ka-chunka-ka-chunk"* in the classic New Orleans style.

Then Haley delivered the last verse, promising that "when the clock strikes twelve, we'll cool off then, start a-rockin' round the clock again....

"We're rock around the clock tonight

We're gonna rock rock rock till broad daylight

We're gonna rock gonna rock around the clock tonight."

At that point Cedrone delivered the song's coda, and once again, since he hadn't been at the rehearsal, he simply recycled the standard descending pattern and walk-up he'd used with Haley on "Rock the Joint" and even earlier, on "Green Tree Boogie." Though it was a common riff for wrapping up a song—at least as old as Earl Fuller's Jazz Band's 1917 hit, "12th Street Rag"—and familiar to any working musician, Cedrone apparently took his inspiration directly from the dynamic, shimmering finale of Les Paul and Mary Ford's 1950 million seller, "How High the Moon."

But the last word, so to speak, was Billy Gussak's flurry of beats on his snare drum. As he would later tell John Haley, Bill's son, "I put that in because I had just done a session the day before where the producer only wanted me to play straight time. I was very frustrated because I always like to throw in something extra.... I made up my mind that at this session I'd get my licks in." As the echo of Gussak's drums faded into the ether, the band members looked searchingly at Gabler in the control room.

"Playback," said the producer, but both he and the engineer knew there were some problems. Sure enough, when Larry McIntire played the tape, the Comets' performance, though excellent, was unusable. To increase the immediacy of "Rock Around the Clock," Gabler had kept urging the engineer to crank up the sound levels, bouncing the volume needle into the red zone to make the recording "hotter." But it was too hot. The instruments had "peaked out," creating some tonal distortion. But worst of all, they'd overpowered Haley. His voice was inaudible.

The musicians groaned. So did Jimmy Myers. The session time was almost up, and another act was already there with his producer, waiting to set up. (Legend has it that Sammy Davis Jr. followed Haley on this occasion, but Davis didn't begin recording for Decca until a couple of months later.) Gabler still needed to get a workable take of this song or else he couldn't release "Thirteen Women," and there wasn't time to rebalance the microphones for another complete take. Thinking quickly, he realized that under-recording Haley on the first take was his salvation. All he had to do was get one more performance of "Rock Around the Clock," at the same tempo as the first take, with the band playing unmiked. Then he could match up the two performances—Haley on one, the band on the other—and bounce them together onto a third tape. Maybe it would work, maybe it wouldn't. But as the minute hand of the clock edged toward the twelve, necessity demanded another try.

"'Rock Around the Clock,' take two."

Everything was exactly the same, except that Gabler had killed every microphone in the room except Haley's, and he was far enough away from the stage that his directional mike would pick up only his voice. The band's performance was only to cue him and keep his exuberance pumping.

The second run-through ended just before the clock struck five. Their studio time was over. "All right, that's a wrap," Gabler announced. He felt as exhausted and dispirited as everyone else in the room. The Comets hurriedly broke down their instruments to get them out of the way, and all but Gussak listlessly packed everything into Haley's Cadillac. Haley and Grande paid the freelance musicians—D'Ambrosio, Lytle, Cedrone, and Gussak—$41.25 apiece, the union scale for a session. It would be the only money the four would ever make from their recording of "Rock Around the Clock."

Gabler walked out of the studio, leaving Larry McIntire and his assistant to rewind the reel-to-reel recording tape and put it away. Tomorrow he'd synchronize the band track with the vocal track, hoping the distortion was minimal enough that he could make the song sound reasonably acceptable. After all, "Rock Around the Clock" was only the B-side. Nobody would pay much attention to it.

The Comets ate supper and waited out the rush-hour traffic before leaving the city. They drove the long, quiet trip back to Chester, listening to an abridged radio version of *Strangers on a Train* on the *Lux Radio Theater*, and arrived home around eleven. Despite his exhaustion, Bill Haley was too depressed and worried to fall asleep for at least an hour. The session had been rushed and the musicians had been tired from the git-go. "Rock Around the Clock" was a washout. He'd blown his first recording session for a major record company.

He didn't know that by a lucky coincidence, as the Comets were sitting on the stage of the Pythian Temple that day, MGM Pictures in Los Angeles, three thousand miles away, was announcing to the Hollywood press that it had just acquired the film rights to an upcoming novel by Evan Hunter called *The Blackboard Jungle*.

CHAPTER 9

WE'LL YELL FOR MORE!

Dubbing together the two performances of "Rock Around the Clock"—the Comets on one take, Haley's voice on the other—onto a new studio tape meant that the final recording would be an extra generation removed from the original, with an attendant loss of fidelity. But as Gabler admitted later, this added layer of duplication "hardened [the recording] up a little bit, gave it an extra something." This new tape was then electronically equalized and compressed to make a tighter, brighter, and less distorted master tape, from which the discs would be cut. Actually, Decca engineers had to make two master tapes each of "Rock Around the Clock" and "Thirteen Women" because the music industry in 1954 inconveniently had to deal with two separate formats for singles: the ten-inch, shellac 78-rpm platter that had been around since the early 1900s, and the seven-inch, vinyl 45-rpm record, introduced only five years earlier, in 1949, by RCA Victor. Though the 45 had better fidelity, it couldn't hold as much volume, especially bass and treble, because its playing area was much smaller and its grooves narrower, so two separate masterings, with different parameters of sound, were required.

On a Thursday, May 6, 1954, Decca Records began shipping copies of "Thirteen Women (And Only One Man in Town)"—Decca 29124 (78) and Decca 9-29124 (45)—to distributors and disc jockeys around the country, in time for the single's official launch the following Monday. Most larger radio stations were already switching over to the lighter, less-breakable 45, so about half of the pink-label promotional copies were in that format, but for regular dark-label records the pressing ratio was about two 78s for every 45. It was one of nine singles Decca put out that week.

Despite Haley's remove of only a few years from his Yodelin' Bill days and the presence of a steel guitar, Milt Gabler didn't have the option of releasing "Thirteen Women" as a hillbilly item. Decca's Nashville fiefdom kept that cornfield all to itself. As Gabler later told writer Rob Finnis, "It was just plugged as a regular record. We just put it out. It wasn't country and western or R&B. It was a regular pop record." Both "Thirteen Women" and its flipside were denoted on the label as "Fox Trot," a sure sign that Decca wasn't certain what it had on its hands. The designation was also a telling comment about the sorry state of American dance music in 1954.

The Fox Trot went back forty years, to when America was awash in dance crazes taken mostly from Harlem vaudeville, like the Black Bottom and Ballin' the Jack. Its roots lay reportedly in a humorous ragtime quickstep introduced

Because of his own financial stake in the song, producer Milt Gabler pushed "Thirteen Women" as the hit side of Bill Haley's first Decca single.

In 1954 only one out of every three "Rock Around the Clock" singles was a 45-rpm record. The rest were 78s. But that would change a year later.

by a white comedian named Harry Fox in 1914. Exhibition dancers streamlined it into a sociable ballroom one-step that any klutz could master. Within three years the Fox Trot was so hot that Victor Records titled the Original Dixieland "Jass" Band's debut disc, the world's first jazz recording, "Livery Stable Blues—Fox Trot." From then on, the term was a catchall for any song with a 4/4 beat. Victor Records even tagged Jimmie Rodgers's groundbreaking 1928 hillbilly hit, "In the Jailhouse Now," as a Fox Trot. That Decca and other companies were still printing "Fox Trot" on their records as late as 1954 shouted the country's need for a new type of dance music.

As the lonely orphan headed off to market, America's six top-selling pop records were Perry Como's "Wanted," Patti Page's "Cross Over the Bridge," Jo

Stafford's "Make Love to Me," Frank Sinatra's "Young at Heart," Kay Starr's "If You Love Me (Really Love Me)," and Nat Cole's "Answer Me, My Love." They were mostly restful and romantic confections from Tin Pan Alley, crooned by holdovers from the 1940s big bands, cushioned in beds of floral violins and chorales, resembling nothing that Bill Haley's Comets were plucking, twanging, thumping, and honking.

Yet there was always a place for novelties on the charts. The Ames Brothers' "Man With the Banjo" was a trite, knee-slapping facsimile of a straw-hat minstrel song, but in the spring of 1954 inveterate whistlers couldn't resist its melodic hook: "Hey, Mr. Banjo, play a song for me." The Four Knights, a black quartet singing in barbershop harmony, had set the country humming along with an anachronism called "Oh, Baby Mine (I Get So Lonely)," based upon the traditional song "Gently Down the Stream," better known as "Row Row Row Your Boat." It must have been the frequent success of oddballs like these, not to mention the sensation that Haley's own "Crazy Man, Crazy" had created the previous year, that gave Milt Gabler an inkling that "Thirteen Women" could compete in the pop market.

The first official announcement was an impressive full-page ad in the May 15, 1954, issue of *Billboard*, the New York–based trade magazine for the entertainment business. Roughly the top forty percent of page 17 was a photo of Decca's new Comets, with Bill Haley's name hailed in large letters. The lower sixty percent was divided into two boxes, with "Thirteen Women"—printed in a tall, rigid, almost foreboding typeface—prominent in the slightly larger box on the left, adorned top and bottom with thirteen stick-figure silhouettes of dancing girls in petticoats. "(We're Gonna) Rock Around the Clock" was on the right, smaller than "Thirteen Women" but printed in a livelier, jumpier font. It seemed to be the fun side.

Elsewhere in the issue, both sides of the single got a mention, as well as the same three-quarter rating, in the "Reviews of New Pop Records" column:

Bill Haley Ork

Thirteen Women 74

Decca 29124—Ops [jukebox operators] *could make good use of a rhythm and blues-ish item about a guy in a town where he's the only man. The beat is strong and Haley sells the lyrics smartly.*

Rock Around the Clock 74

Big beat and repetitious blues lyric makes this a good attempt at "cat music" and one which should grab coin in the right locations.

As far as Decca producer Milt Gabler was concerned, "Rock Around the Clock" (seen here on 78) was the throwaway B-side of the record.

As so often happened in those days, when many disc jockeys listened to all the records that came into their stations and had some choice over which ones they put on the air, several of them flipped the record over and played the more exciting B-side. Listeners began asking for "Rock Around the Clock" on the station request lines or at the local record stores. They played it on neighborhood jukeboxes. As distributors began reordering singles, they asked for "Rock Around the Clock" instead of "Thirteen Women," alerting the New York sales staff that they'd been leaning on the wrong side of the record. Two weeks after the single's first appearance in *Billboard*, Decca's new full-page ad for its latest round of singles relegated "Thirteen Women" to insignificance, barely legible beneath the proclamation: "Rock Around the Clock." A few pages later,

The 1954 Comets were (clockwise from top) Bill Haley, Dick Richards, Marshall Lytle, Joey D'Ambrosio, Johnny Grande, and Billy Williamson.

the magazine's "This Week's Best Buys" section, based on sales reports in key markets, reported optimistically: "Northern operators have been doing excellent business with this disc since it was released two or three weeks ago. Reports from New England, New York, Philadelphia, Pittsburgh, Cincinnati, Milwaukee, Cleveland and St. Louis have been especially good. Flip is 'Thirteen Women.'"

But the single stalled before it could get a head of steam. Though Decca continued to promote "Rock Around the Clock" until mid-June, it charted for only one week (No. 23) at the end of May and did a fast fade after selling, by Gabler's estimate, about 75,000 copies—a fairly respectable showing but nothing special for an artist who'd had a No. 12 hit the previous year. Perhaps the time wasn't right. Or maybe Decca was concentrating its best efforts behind Kitty Kallen's "Little Things Mean a Lot," which leapt atop the national charts on June 5 and stayed there until July 24, when another Decca single, the Four Aces' "Three Coins in the Fountain" (released on the same day as "Rock Around the Clock"), took its place.

By then the group, including Danny Cedrone, had already returned to the Pythian Temple in early June to record two more numbers for a follow-up single. Billy Gussak wasn't available for this session, so Gabler called in drummer David "Panama" Francis, a black veteran of the Cab Calloway and Lucky Millinder bands. The obligatory Jimmy Myers property for the session was a lightweight novelty called "A.B.C. Boogie," written by a couple of his Philadelphia hirelings. For the A-side, Gabler and Haley decided to do another cover recording, this time of a song already climbing the R&B charts.

Atlantic Records had recorded Big Joe Turner's "Shake, Rattle, and Roll" four months earlier, in February, and released it on April 12 as the Comets were in the studio cutting "Rock Around the Clock." The song's official composer was Atlantic's veteran black record producer, Jesse Stone, under the pseudonym Charles Calhoun. He said later that he used the expression "shake, rattle, and roll" as a way of tying together the disjointed, often shopworn blues lyrics that Turner had been singing in black nightclubs for more than twenty years. Very likely its roots lie in a 1919 "coon" song, "Shake, Rattle and Roll (Who's Got Me)," a tale of a craps shooter—"When I shake, rattle and roll [the dice], it sounds like melody, I've got four bits more that says I'll pass, who's got me?"— recorded by a popular white blackface singer, Al Bernard, for Thomas Edison's gramophone company. But "shake, rattle, and roll" also carried sexual overtones. For example, on a 1931 blues recording called "Shake, Mattie," Kansas Joe McCoy sang, "Shake, shake on, Mattie, shake, rattle, and roll, I can't get enough now to satisfy my soul. Well shake it, Mattie, shake shake on the bone, every time she shake now, another dollar gone."

Joe Turner's "Shake, Rattle, and Roll" was likewise suggestive—certainly more so than Dickie Thompson's "Thirteen Women and One Man." For example, Turner sang, "Wearin' low dresses, sun comes shinin' through ... girl, I can't believe all that mess belongs to you." In another line he likened himself to "a one-eyed cat peepin' in a seafood store," and in yet another he vamped, "Over the hill, way down underneath...girl, you make me grit my teeth." Obviously some changes had to be made before Gabler could ready the song for pop radio. The "wearin' low dresses" verse was the first to go, replaced by "Wearing those dresses, your hair done up so nice." Another line, "I believe to my soul you're the devil in nylon hose," became "I believe you're doing me wrong and now I know." The "over the hill" line was omitted altogether. Yet neither Haley nor Gabler caught the meaning of the seafood-loving one-eyed cat, or simply chose to leave it in because they wanted a connection to "cat music"—a term *Billboard* was already using as a euphemism for R&B.

When the session was over, the Comets left New York and went back out on the road, scrambling from one job to another. It had been a year since "Crazy Man, Crazy" left the charts. Drummer Dick Richards told writer David Hirschberg, "Lord Jim [Ferguson] tells us to come down to Florida, he's lined up a string of bookings. We'd spent our last dime to get down there, then he tells us, 'Sorry, fellas, the deal fell through.' We only got paid when we were working, so we had no money to go home. Jim didn't care—he went down with his mother and was eating in the fancy restaurants. He'd sit by the window and wave at us outside. We had hardly enough to share a bowl of chili between us."

A 1919 "coon" song called "Shake Rattle and Roll," written and recorded by Al Bernard, was probably the root of Big Joe Turner's 1954 hit.

American-International Pictures discovered the teenage film market in 1956 with Shake, Rattle and Rock!, *starring Big Joe Turner (above) and Fats Domino. Despite the similarity of the movie's title, Turner didn't perform his hit song, "Shake, Rattle, and Roll."*

The only person who would book them was a club owner—but not in his main room. "He had a back room in his place that he never used, and said if we'd clean the place up he'd let us play for a percentage of the take. We had nothing else. So we went in there—it was a real mess. We cleaned the whole place out, built a stage for us—we made a room for this guy. Then, right after we opened, 'Shake, Rattle, and Roll' made its way into the jukebox in the main room. We were on our way."

Almost overnight the Comets streaked back into the big time. "Shake, Rattle, and Roll" entered the charts on August 21, shot to No. 7, and spent a total of twenty-seven weeks—half a year—in the Top 40. Even Turner's original version, caught up in the maelstrom of the Comets' success, sold enough copies to shimmy over from the R&B charts and reach No. 22 pop. In October, Universal-International Pictures filmed the group for *Round Up of Rhythm*— a "short subject" that opened for Hollywood movies in theaters around the country. The Comets, with Haley playing lead guitar, displayed their dynamic stage act in a live set, performing "Crazy Man, Crazy," Joey D'Ambrosio's

"Strait Jacket," and "Shake, Rattle, and Roll." "Rock Around the Clock" was nowhere in sight.

Decca packaged the Comets' first two singles into an extended-play 45, or EP, called *Shake, Rattle and Roll*. An EP in those days was a semi-album because it contained half of what was packaged in a standard ten-inch, eight-song LP. A few months later, in early 1955, the company put the Comets' first four singles on an album, also called *Shake, Rattle and Roll*, using the same cartoon cover as the EP. "Rock Around the Clock" was naturally part of the album, but the liner notes mentioned it only in passing as Haley's first Decca single, "a tune included in the present selection." As far as Decca, the Comets, and their fans were concerned, "Rock Around the Clock" was water under the bridge, a small hit that had never taken off, but still a lively show number.

On July 17, 1954, ten days after the "Shake, Rattle, and Roll" session, the Comets lost their studio guitarist, Danny Cedrone. On a late-night errand to get his wife a sandwich, he fell down the steps of a friend's upstairs restaurant in Philadelphia and died instantly from a broken neck, never knowing that he had laid down the first recognizable guitar solo of rock 'n' roll—the granddaddy of countless thousands to follow. Those eight bars of fancy flight, more than any other, determined that the guitar, not the saxophone, would dominate this new music as it evolved from rhythm and blues.

Decca's first Comets album, released in 1954 on the heels of the hit single "Shake, Rattle, and Roll," contained the group's first four singles (eight songs in all). Like most pop albums that year, it was a ten-inch record.

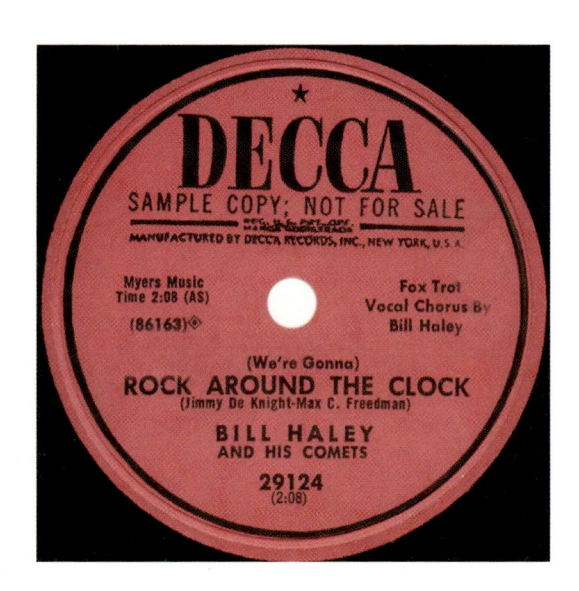

Major record companies usually sent specially colored promotional singles to disc jockeys. Decca's were mostly pink. Note the change in Decca's logo between 1954 (the 78 at the top) and 1955 (the 45).

98

The Comets' first extended-play (EP) record in 1954 was a half-album, with the same cover and title as the simultaneously released, ten-inch long-play album, but with only half the tracks.

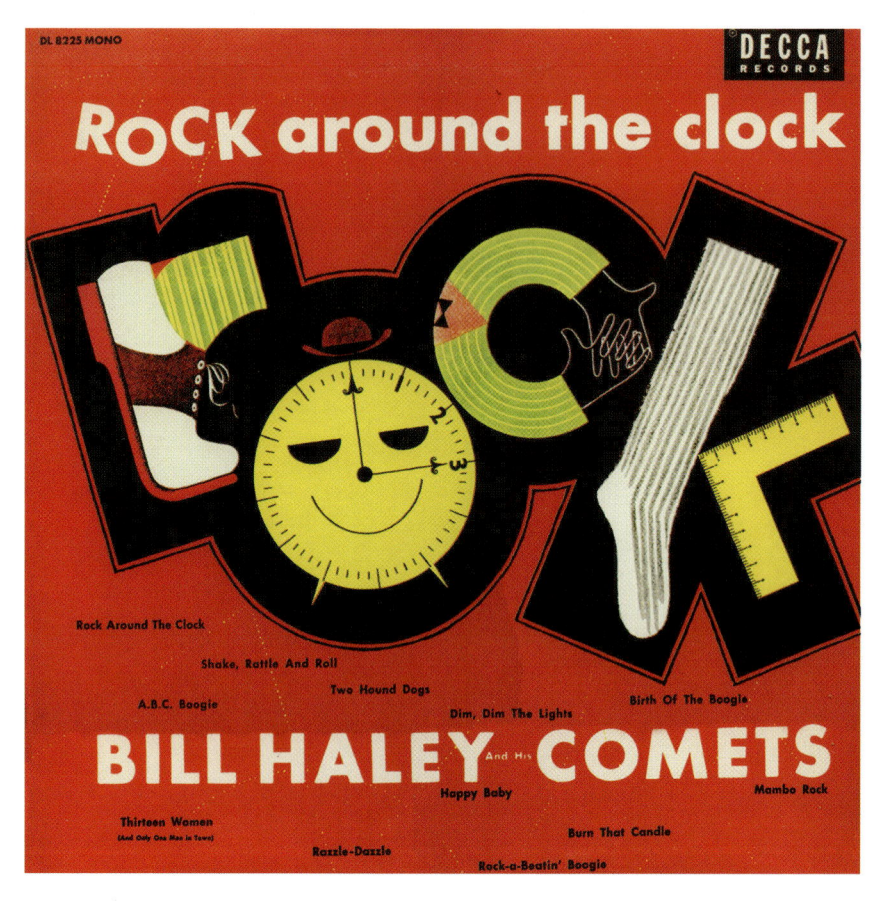

Decca reissued the Comets' 1954 album a year later as a 12-inch LP (above). Four songs were added and the cover was changed to capitalize on the tremendous popularity of "Rock Around the Clock."

Though the Comets left Essex Records in early 1954, bootleggers pressed copies of "Rock Around the Clock" on the company's imprint in 1955, with "Crazy Man, Crazy" on the B-side. The single remains popular with collectors.

British Decca—which was a separate entity unaffiliated with American Decca—released Bill Haley and His Comets' "Rock Around the Clock" in the United Kingdom in 1954. The single's sales were negligible.

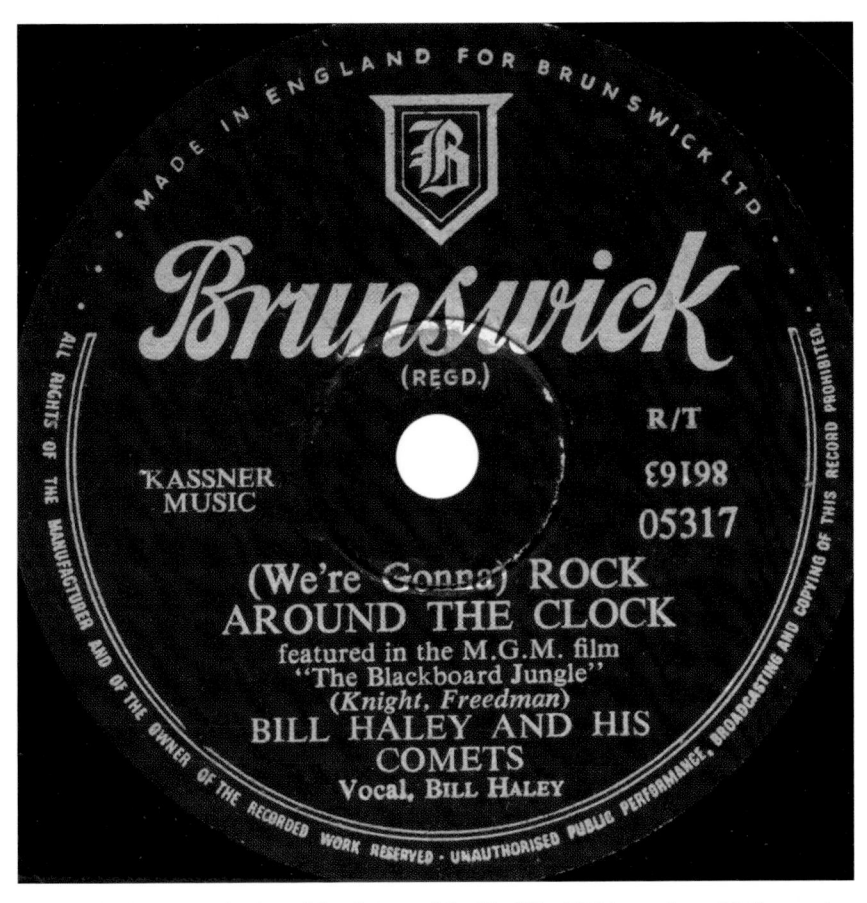

When British Brunswick reissued "Rock Around the Clock" in 1955 in tandem with the country-wide opening of the film Blackboard Jungle, *the single shot to the top of the U.K. record charts.*

As late as 1957, rock 'n' roll music had retained enough of its exotic appeal that True Strange *magazine (with Bill Haley and Elvis Presley on the cover) likened it to the pagan rhythms of primitive African tribes.*

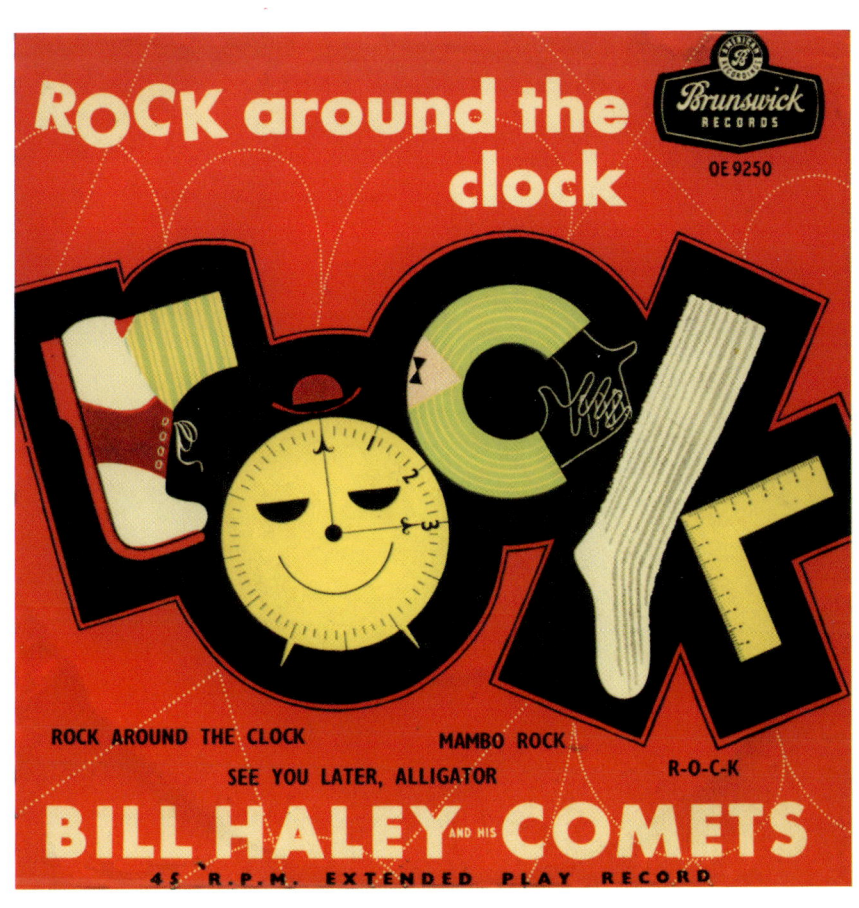

In the United Kingdom, Brunswick Records duplicated the cover artwork from American Decca's 1955 Rock Around the Clock *album for both its EP and LP releases there. In the U.S. Decca reissued its 1954 "jalopy"-cover EP.*

The Comets' 1955 French EP highlighted the connection between the song "Rock Around the Clock" and the popular film Blackboard Jungle, *released there as* Graine de Violence (Seeds of Violence).

The French label CID used a hint of sex and violence on the cover of the Comets' Rock Around the Clock *album to underscore the title song's inclusion in* Blackboard Jungle (Graine de Violence).

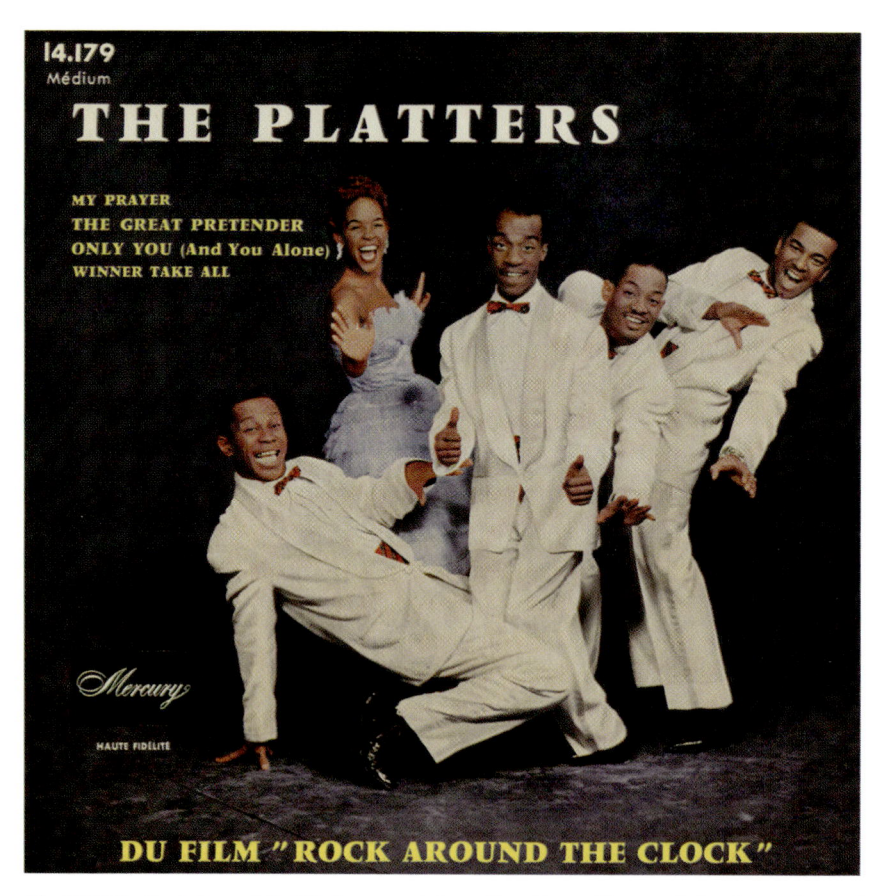

The 1956 film Rock Around the Clock *was an international box-office smash that boosted record sales around the world for its three rock 'n' roll acts, including the Platters, who were popular in France.*

In 1955 Brazilian Decca reissued the 1954 eight-song Shake, Rattle, and Roll *album on a ten-inch disc. Its jacket blazoned scenes from* Blackboard Jungle, *released in Brazil as* Sementes De Violência (Seeds of Violence).

In 1956 Brazilian Decca reissued the 1955 American 12-inch Rock Around the Clock *album (Ao Balanço Das Horas) in conjunction with the film of the same title. Bill Haley and His Comets later toured Brazil.*

In 1956 the Festival label in Australia and New Zealand repackaged the Comets' 1955 album for the release of the film Rock Around the Clock. *Early the following year, the group's Australian tour was a huge success.*

In 1955 Argentina Decca reissued the Comets' ten-inch 1954 Shake, Rattle, and Roll *album, complete with the original cover, as* Bailando el Rock (Dance the Rock).

CHAPTER 10

BLACKBOARD JUNGLE

Richard Brooks, a forty-two-year-old Hollywood screenwriter and director, was driving home from a poker game late one night, exhausted and maybe a little depressed. Metro-Goldwyn-Mayer Studios in Culver City, where he was under contract, had just saddled him with a film project he despised, a remake of the silent sword-and-sandals epic, *Ben-Hur*, based on Lew Wallace's nineteenth-century novel. Facing Monday morning with dread, Brooks was barely listening to the radio haphazardly tuned to a midnight-to-dawn program. Suddenly a record came on that was unlike anything he'd ever heard, rocking and careening with such chaotic energy that it yanked him out of his distraction and into the exhilaration of the perfect moment, as scented night breezes fluttered across his face and through his hair. He didn't catch the title, he said many years later, but for the next several days he couldn't get the song's beat out of his head.

At the studio, as good luck would have it, Brooks ran into veteran director William Wyler, who was also disgusted with his latest assignment. "It's this shit about juvenile delinquents," Wyler complained. Some novel called *The Blackboard Jungle* that hadn't even been published yet—MGM had bought the galley proofs—about a teacher dealing with teenage thugs at a vocational high school in New York City.

Brooks, a former Philadelphia street kid who'd made his bones in the late forties writing gritty noir films like *Key Largo*, liked the sound of it. He suggested to Wyler that they trade projects, even though *Ben-Hur* was slated to be a major picture and *The Blackboard Jungle*—whose title would be shortened to *Blackboard Jungle*—was budgeted as a B movie. The older man agreed.

"So I was writing the [*Blackboard Jungle*] screenplay and began to think back about this music I had heard on the car radio," Brooks later told writer J.D. Marshall. "It seemed so right for it." He visited a couple of record shops, but none of the clerks could identify what he was looking for. He wasn't sure if the artists were black or white. Finally he dropped by Wallich's Music City, a popular store on the corner of Sunset and Vine that stocked the newest, hippest recordings because it was just down the block from Hollywood's music publishers' row. The clerk asked him, "Where'd you hear it?"

"It was way up around 1500 somewhere."

Screenwriter-director Richard Brooks (seen here in the 1960s) claimed that he set much of the pacing and rhythm of Blackboard Jungle *to the beat of Bill Haley's "Rock Around the Clock."*

"It probably was a station where they played black music," said the clerk. "Do you remember how it sounded, do you remember any words, how was it?"

Brooks sang what little he recalled: "One-two-three o'clock, four o'clock rock."

"Let me find out."

"He called about two weeks later," said Brooks. "He said, 'Yeah, there is a record like that, but it died—they played it for about a week—you want that record? I'll call the station if you want'…. So he got this 78 record, and I used to play it all day while I was writing the screenplay."

Brooks claimed that when he began shooting *Blackboard Jungle* on the MGM lot in the middle of November 1954, he played "Rock Around the Clock" during some of the high school scenes "so the kids would begin to walk to that rhythm, work to that rhythm." He told film critic Judith Crist, "We played the record every day. The kids rocked to it, danced to it." Bill Haley's voice occasionally ended up in the dailies—the takes of each scene reviewed late that evening or early the next morning by producer Pandro Berman and MGM's production chief, Dore Schary. One day Schary sent Brooks a memo demanding, "Will you throw that goddamn piece of music out. I can't watch the dailies—it's killing me with this goddamned music!"

Ironically, in Evan Hunter's novel the young toughs at the manual trades high school favored the type of mellow pop music antithetical to Bill Haley and His Comets. In a scene where several students trash a teacher's collection of early jazz and big band 78s, they demand to know why he isn't playing cool vocalists like Perry Como, Tony Bennett, and the Hilltoppers. "Ain't you got nothing good on that goddamn box?" Hunter wrote. "How about Julius La Rosa? Now he's got something on the ball. Or how about Joni James?" Nobody expected that many teenagers would soon consider these artists as dated as Rudy Vallee, thanks to "Rock Around the Clock"—not even Richard Brooks, for when he finished shooting in late December and began to edit the film, he took his lead from the novel's more refined choice of music and told Berman he wanted to hire a young hotshot composer, André Previn, to write the score. The producer shook his head. *Blackboard Jungle* was "too little" for Previn. "You've got a B movie here, forget it. I don't want to spend any money on the music for this thing."

Brooks countered by going back into Berman's office waving his "Rock Around the Clock" 78. "Well, let's buy *this* record then." When MGM inquired about the "synchronization" rights for "Rock Around the Clock," Decca

Records was happy to make a generous offer: $5,000 for three plays in the picture. Or $7,500 for all rights. MGM could own the recording outright if it wanted.

According to Brooks, Berman said, "Well, let's just buy the record for $5,000 and the hell with it. It's not worth the other $2,500." (This is the same Pandro Berman who in 1962 would insert an orchestral version of "Rock Around the Clock" into another film, *The Reluctant Debutante*.)

It should be pointed out that some of the details of the late Richard Brooks's various recollections about *Blackboard Jungle* don't always jibe with each other or with what others remembered. Jimmy Myers, not the most reliable source, credited himself for getting "Rock Around the Clock" into the movie by sending 45s to his many contacts at studios around Hollywood. According to several accounts, either Brooks or Berman heard his daughter playing the record on her phonograph, but Brooks didn't have any children at

Blackboard Jungle stars Anne Francis and Glenn Ford peruse Evan Hunter's original novel. The pop music that Hunter's fictional high school students were listening to became passé after "Rock Around the Clock."

Peter Ford, seen here on the Columbia Pictures lot with his father Glenn in 1961, says Blackboard Jungle director Richard Brooks first heard "Rock Around the Clock" during one of his visits to the Ford home.

the time, and Berman's two daughters later said they'd never heard the record until their father played it for them.

More feasible is the claim of Peter Ford, the son of actor Glenn Ford and dancer Eleanor Powell, that he was an R&B-obsessed fifth-grader blasting "Rock Around the Clock" on the hi-fi in his family's music den—the same room where former resident Max Steiner had composed the scores of *Gone With the Wind*, *Casablanca*, and many other classic films—when Brooks showed up one evening to talk to his dad about the upcoming production. Ford says, "Mr. Brooks was so impressed when he heard my 78 that he borrowed it and never brought it back. The next thing I knew, 'Rock Around the Clock' was playing in *Blackboard Jungle*." Neither Joel Freeman, the film's assistant director, nor actor Jamie Farr, who played one of the students, recalls Brooks spinning the Haley record on the set during production. "We didn't have that song until the film was almost completed," Freeman said recently. Given the tricky nature of memory, who's to say what actually happened in detail? But since Brooks was responsible for getting the song into his picture, we'll have to go with his account until enough evidence turns up to suggest otherwise.

He placed "Rock Around the Clock" at the very beginning of *Blackboard Jungle*, blaring over the credits, then bleeding into the first scene as an idealistic young teacher (Glenn Ford) enters the courtyard of North Manual High School in the Bronx, where working-class kids are jitterbugging, nodding, and, in one case, banging a trash can lid to the beat of the music—all perfectly synchronized since the actors supposedly had been listening to the record. To accentuate the film's underlying theme that urban American kids had become like wild animals, several students are reaching their arms through the steel bars of a fence separating the school from the street and snapping their fingers to the song's jungle rhythm.

In order to make Bill Haley's recording cover all this ground, Brooks stretched it beyond its original two minutes and eight seconds by duping the second instrumental break—the amped-up vamp with everybody wailing along with Joey D'Ambrosio's honking saxophone—and inserting it right up front, after Bill Haley's first vocal verse. This edited version, with the instrumental chorus appearing twice, plays again at the end of the film. The song "Rock Around the Clock" also appears, almost subliminally, as a Stan Kentonesque jazz number, with screaming brass and a pounding drum solo, during the film's most brutal scene, as Glenn Ford and a fellow teacher are attacked and beaten in a dark alley by several students. This reconfiguration of "Rock Around the Clock," arranged by musical director Charles Wolcott and credited to the MGM Orchestra, was later released on MGM Records.

After uneventful test screenings in the upscale Los Angeles suburb of Encino on February 27, 1955, and in Hollywood a day later, MGM opened *Blackboard Jungle* at two Loew's Theaters, one in Boston, the other in Manhattan's Times Square, on March 19, a Saturday. The film immediately attracted the press. Bosley Crowther, an influential critic for *The New York Times*, called it "one of the toughest, hardest hitting social dramas the screen has had in years. In picturing the shocking experience of a young man teaching in a city vocational high school, where he is up against a classroom full of rowdies, hoodlums and outright juvenile crooks, it creates a terrifying notion of the indiscipline and rebelliousness of slum-area youth and the almost inability on the part of teachers to handle them." Crowther seemed offended by *Blackboard Jungle*'s "bloodcurdling, nightmarish" realism because "if the details in this film are 'stacked' and exaggerated...it seems to us irresponsible and fraught with peril."

Juvenile delinquent Vic Morrow (standing) challenges the authority of teacher Glenn Ford in Blackboard Jungle. *The film's controversial black co-star, Sidney Poitier, is sitting near the center of the photo.*

Given the fears of the day, *Blackboard Jungle* was certain to hit a nerve. The media had already grafted the words "juvenile" and "delinquency" together in the public's mind. Children born just before World War II were coming of age. Their fathers had been off fighting or otherwise engaged in the war effort; their mothers had gone to work in the factories, leaving the kids home to raise themselves. Now social pundits were branding them a lost generation. The little ingrates didn't know or care that their parents had undergone years of privations just to save them from the fascists. An alarming 1954 FBI report gathered from a thousand American towns and cities disclosed that kids under eighteen had been responsible for more than 53 percent of car thefts, nearly 50 percent of burglaries, 18 percent of robberies, and 16 percent of rapes in 1953. FBI Director J. Edgar Hoover added, "The nation can expect an appalling increase in the number of crimes that will be committed by teenagers in the years ahead unless the crime rate among juveniles can be lowered." Even President Eisenhower, during his State of the Union message in early 1955, declared an

CHAPTER 10: Blackboard Jungle   **119**

emergency: "To help the states do a better job, we must strengthen their resources for preventing and dealing with juvenile delinquency. I shall propose federal legislation to assist the states in dealing with this nationwide problem."

In those days most cities had licensing bureaus whose job, besides issuing permits, was to sanction all public entertainment in case it exceeded the limits of decency or propriety. In other words, they acted as censors. The most famous office was Boston's Licensing Division which, in its zeal to make sure the girls at the local burlesque houses didn't lose their pasties, had popularized the expression "Banned in Boston." Thanks to Hollywood's self-policing Hays Office, city regulators only rarely interfered with movie content, usually in matters of religious sensibilities. But when *Blackboard Jungle* went into nationwide release in April, its explosive and seditious appeal to teenagers changed the rules—as if they were members of terrorist cells awaiting their marching orders. In Memphis the mayor and the city commission restricted theater admissions to adults. Milwaukee demanded that four "objectionable" scenes be cut before the movie could open there. Schenectady shut down the film during its opening week for inciting a gang fight and other teenage hooliganism. In June, William Mooring, an editor with *Tidings*, a Catholic magazine, went before Estes

A brassy jazz version of "Rock Around the Clock" by the MGM Orchestra blared over Blackboard Jungle's *most violent scene, as teenage thugs beat up two teachers, including Glenn Ford, in a dark alley.*

Kefauver's Senate Juvenile Delinquency Subcommittee to decry the film's degeneracy: "Unless there is a change in the direction pictures are taking, we may find ourselves plunged into new horrors of sexual aberration."

What made it a *cause célèbre*, however, was its banishment from Atlanta by the city's censor, a forty-four-year-old alderman's wife who declared that *Blackboard Jungle* was "immoral, obscene, licentious and will adversely affect the peace, health, morals and good order of this city." MGM's parent company, Loew's Inc.—hinting to the media that the Southern lady was outraged primarily by a leading character being an insolent and defiant young Negro (Sidney Poitier)—hurried into the local U.S. District Court to enjoin Atlanta from enforcing the ban because it violated their First Amendment right to freedom of the press. The city, fearful both of being labeled racist and of having its licensing board challenged on legal grounds, hastily backed down.

Richard Brooks recalled being invited by Joseph Schenck, Loew's chairman of the board, to the company offices overlooking Times Square. "My boy," said the aging mogul, "look down there at the theater. It's eleven o'clock in the morning, it's raining, and people are standing in line to see your movie. Why are they standing in line? Why do they like this movie?"

Blackboard Jungle was indeed a box office smash. At a time when the price of admission was, at most, thirty-five cents, the $360,000 film grossed four million dollars over the spring and summer of 1955. Then, as Loew's International, the company's overseas arm, began distributing *Blackboard Jungle* around the world, it garnered more bad press guaranteed to put more warm butts into the seats. In the United Kingdom it got an "X" certificate that kept kids under sixteen out of the theaters. Japan called it "a harmful movie" and refused to allow teenagers under eighteen to see it. So did Israel. Several countries, including India, Egypt, and Uruguay, initially banned the film altogether. But Loew's' biggest public relations coup came in September when Clare Boothe Luce, the U.S. Ambassador to Italy, refused to attend the Venice Film Festival unless it withdrew *Blackboard Jungle* from its schedule. Without having seen the picture, she accused it of creating a "seriously distorted impression of American youth and American schools" and bolstering "Italian Communist anti-U.S. propaganda." The U.S. State Department upheld her objection and brushed aside Loew's' charges of political censorship; Mrs. Luce had merely exercised her right not to attend the festival. *Blackboard Jungle* was yanked, and the international outcry was priceless. By May 1957, the *Hollywood Reporter* would announce that the film had grossed $8 million all

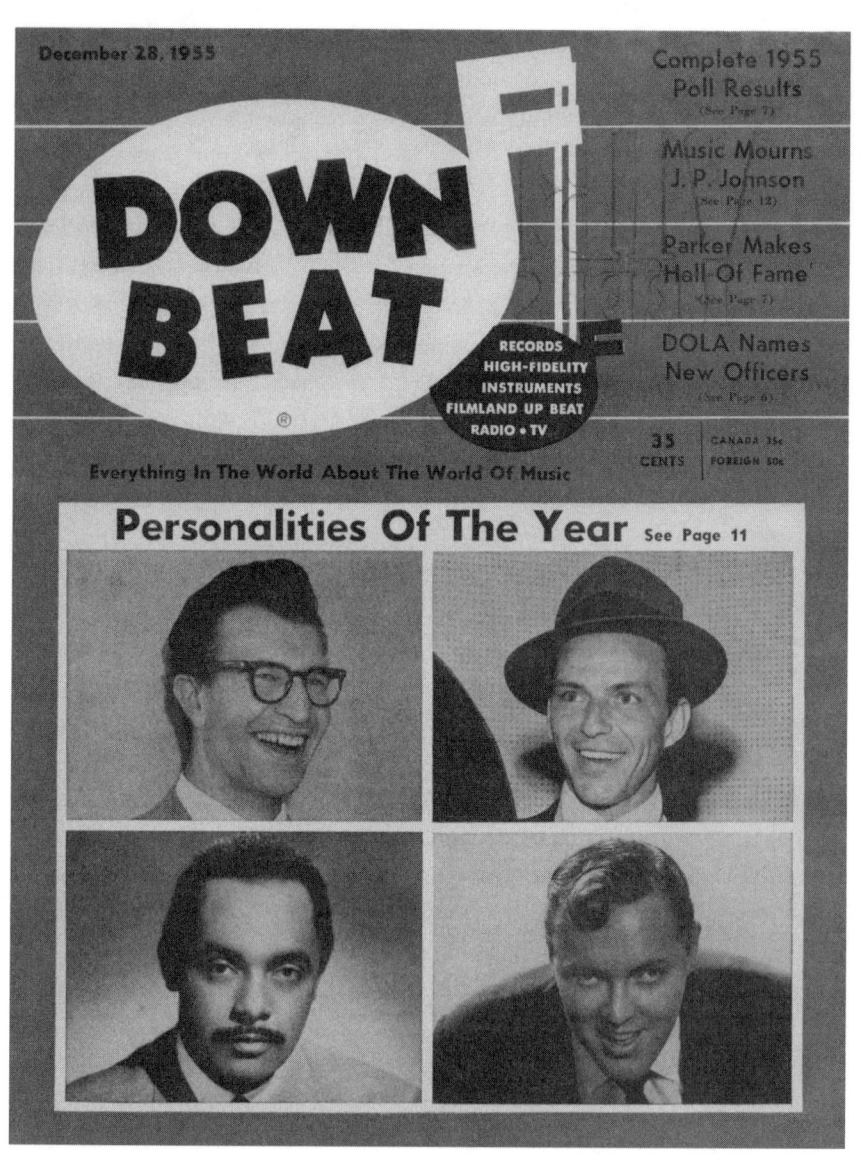

In its end-of-the-year wrap-up, Down Beat *magazine dubbed Bill Haley the top-selling R&B artist of 1955 and put him on the cover with Dave Brubeck, Frank Sinatra, and Perez Prado.*

over the world during the previous two years and was still drawing audiences in foreign markets.

For Hollywood, the stir over *Blackboard Jungle* and several lesser hard-edged social dramas that year was a valuable lesson in how to create what historian Daniel Boorstin, just six years later, would call the "pseudo event," a postmodern concoction designed to make front-page news even though it had no significance or basis in reality. Though there were isolated incidents of teenagers getting rowdy during screenings, in most cases they were simply kids being kids, clapping their hands, dancing in the aisles, refusing to be quiet, and yelling at the theater manager if he stopped the movie out of fear that things might get out of hand, just like it said in the newspapers. If cops arrived in a show of force to make sure nothing happened, it became a news story—especially if they overzealously provoked any defiance from the kids—and provided unlimited, self-generating publicity for *Blackboard Jungle*.

Though nobody seemed fully aware of it at the time, the film also signaled a sea change in Hollywood movie making. The growing popularity of television in the early fifties—highlighted in 1953 by a national craze for Swanson's new portable, frozen "TV Dinner" that moved family suppers into the living room in front of the cathode-ray tube—had dovetailed disastrously with the major film studios being forced by a U.S. Justice Department anti-trust lawsuit to divest themselves of their theater chains. Without a reliable filmgoing audience or a circuit of assured nationwide bookings, the studios could no longer maintain the expense of an assembly line, which in turn made it less profitable to keep expensive stars under long-term contracts. They desperately tried to lure people back into theaters with wide-screen Cinerama in 1952 and eye-popping 3-D a year later, but with only modest success.

Several canny independent producers, however, noted that teenagers had not abandoned the movies. Nor were they discerning about production values as long as there were attractive young actors, hot music, hot cars, a little sex, and maybe a monster or two. In 1954 Samuel Arkoff and James Nicholson founded American International Pictures with the novel idea of making cheap exploitation flicks for a young audience. That same year, Columbia Pictures released a surprise hit called *The Wild One*, about two motorcycle gangs in World War II leather bomber jackets terrorizing a small California town. Hollywood's good-natured adolescents like Henry Aldridge and Andy Hardy had driven their flivvers off into the sunset, replaced by a sullen Marlon Brando draped astride a Triumph Thunderbird motorcycle, answering the question, "Hey, what are *you* rebelling against, Johnny?" with "Whattaya got?" Teenagers anxious to escape their parents' TV dens and watch impudent reflections of themselves defying authority flocked to the movie theaters and drive-ins wherever it played.

Blackboard Jungle, released a full year later, was *The Wild One* transposed

The September 1955 issue of Hit Parader, *released earlier in the summer, showcased the Comets and printed the lyrics of "Rock Around the Clock." By September, three members of the group on the cover were gone.*

into the big city—but with a rock 'n' roll introduction instead of *The Wild One*'s "cool jazz" soundtrack. MGM was excited enough about the teenage appeal of "Rock Around the Clock" that it prominently used the recording as a selling point in *Blackboard Jungle*'s trailer, blaring over several of the film's most menacing images of young toughs on the prowl, as a voice intoned, "You're listening to 'Rock Around the Clock'...."

Though film reviewers mentioned "Rock Around the Clock" only in passing, if at all, it astonished everyone in the audience. The drum intro and Haley's dramatic count up the clock cracked through the theater in total darkness, then the band throbbed through the large speakers that not even a good jukebox could match. Very few recordings ever got that kind of a super audio introduction without parents yelling, "Turn that damn thing down!" It was like the heralding of important news. Evan Hunter later said, "The movie fed the record, the record fed the movie."

As it turned out, 1955 was a great year for popular films pushing songs high into the charts. During *Blackboard Jungle*'s first two months in the theaters,

After the breakout successes of both "Rock Around the Clock" and Blackboard Jungle, *MGM released its own big-band soundtrack version of the song, performed in the brassy styles of Stan Kenton and Count Basie.*

CHAPTER 10: Blackboard Jungle 125

only three songs—"The Ballad of Davy Crockett," "Unchained Melody," and "Cherry Pink (And Apple Blossom White)"—occupied *Billboard*'s No. 1 slot, and all three were movie themes. (Walt Disney's *Davy Crockett, King of the Wild Frontier* actually aired first in serial form on TV before an abridged version opened in theaters.) But none of them sounded remotely like "Rock Around the Clock."

More importantly, none of them carried the electrical political charge that the Comets' recording got from its association with *Blackboard Jungle*. Though the film was ostensibly on the side of good manners and civil order (embodied in the Glenn Ford character, Richard Dadier), its subtext of American society's indifference toward poor and blue-collar students sympathized with their resentment at being shunted into a run-down vocational school and fast-tracked into, at best, a lifetime of numbing and joyless labor. Even most of their teachers had written them off. Their anger was palpable throughout the film, ready to ignite at any moment, transforming "Rock Around the Clock" from an amusing novelty to a Greek chorus for adolescent rebellion. Implicit in all the news stories of spontaneous outbursts of vandalism inside and outside the nation's movie theaters was that "Rock Around the Clock" supplied the driving tempo for kids slicing seats with switchblades and running in hordes into the streets to terrorize good citizens.

Shortly after *Blackboard Jungle* premiered, Richard Brooks got a call from a friend in Boston telling him there was no sound during the first reel. Brooks immediately phoned the theater manager to ask what was going on. The man replied, "We don't turn on the sound until the second reel."

"Are you insane?"

"But it's that music," the manager insisted. "They get up in the aisles and dance." He was afraid that their stomping might collapse the balcony of his aging Beaux Arts–era theater. Almost from the start, "Rock Around the Clock" was threatening to bring down an entire tradition of American entertainment.

CHAPTER 11

ROCK AROUND THE CLOCK AGAIN

On April 17, 1955, before the *Blackboard Jungle* storm broke, Bill Haley and His Comets headlined disc jockey Bill Randle's rhythm and blues show at the Masonic Temple in Cleveland, Ohio. Though Alan Freed is now Cleveland's most storied radio huckster from that era, Bill Randle, who aired locally on station WERE and syndicated his show on New York City's WCBS, was nearly as important in promoting early rock 'n' roll. Randle lacked Freed's manic energy and jivey patter, but he was more amenable to playing white artists if they sounded like cool cats. He became Elvis Presley's first northern champion, significant enough in RCA Victor's game plan that when Presley made his national television debut on the Dorsey Brothers' *Stage Show* on January 28, 1956, Randle was on hand to introduce him. He also produced a film with Presley and Bill Haley, but more on that later.

Thanks to Randle's Masonic Temple recording, we can listen in on what a typical Comets stage show sounded like before "Rock Around the Clock" changed everything. Haley and the boys were promoting their latest recording—a modest two-sided hit, "Mambo Rock" and "Birth of the Boogie"—but they also presented a mixed bag of hillbilly, R&B, and pop music, interspersed with barn-dance humor.

Marshall Lytle took over vocal duties on the Dominoes' "That's What You're Doing to Me" and on his own song, "Let's All Rock Together," which he would later record after he left the Comets. Dick Richards crooned a hammy "Ol' Man River" and Billy Williamson sang "Big Mamou," Link Davis's 1952 Cajun song.

Joey D'Ambrosio romped and wailed through two instrumentals. And Haley, Richards, and Williamson, harmonizing as a trio, did a jumped-up rendition of a thirties Tin Pan Alley trifle called "I've Told Ev'ry Little Star."

By the time the group got around to "Rock Around the Clock," Haley introduced it almost in passing as "a song that's featured in the MGM picture *The Blackboard Jungle*," then delivered it with the same enthusiasm—no more, no less—he gave the other numbers in the Comets' repertoire. If anyone in the audience had been inspired to run out and grab a copy of the single, they might not have been able to find it. Even though the trade papers had announced three months earlier, in February, that Decca and two other record companies had back-catalog songs on the soundtrack of the upcoming *Blackboard Jungle*, Decca didn't get around to reissuing "Rock Around the Clock" until April, a couple of weeks after the film's release, just as "Mambo Rock" was beginning to falter on the charts.

If any new music seemed ready to break wide open in early 1955, it was the mambo, an Afro-Cuban dance rhythm from the nineteenth century that had arrived on New York's shores with Cuban bandleader Perez Prado around 1950. Four years later, everybody from R&B queen Ruth Brown ("Mambo Baby") to Perry Como ("Papa Loves Mambo") was recording mambo songs. "A few months ago it would have been a shock had these labels issued a mambo with a top pop singer," *Billboard* said in September 1954. "Today it is taken as a matter of course." Though LaVern Baker's R&B million-seller, "Tweedlee Dee," didn't mention the dance by name, it was a full-on mambo, right down to the drummer rapping the Latin beat on a cowbell. Even the Comets' "Thirteen Women" had contained a mambo reference. No wonder Haley, in early 1955, decided to wed the mambo with the other musical fad of the moment, rock 'n' roll, in "Mambo Rock." When all was said and done, he was still a dance caller, urging the audience to get up and move around the floor. And when teenagers soundly rejected the mambo later in the year, Haley just as quickly dropped it.

"Rock Around the Clock," reissued with its 1954 catalog number, got its first push in San Francisco, where early radio play made it a "Territorial Best Seller" in mid-April. By the first week of May it was number one in Buffalo and getting heavy airplay in the Baltimore-Washington area, New Orleans, Cleveland, and Denver. In the week ending May 18 "Rock Around the Clock" entered *Billboard*'s twenty-song "Honor Roll of Hits" at No. 17. The publication's music industry tabulations showed that it was getting only modest radio play and almost no jukebox action, yet it rated No. 10 in the "Best Sellers in Stores" chart, indicating that *Blackboard Jungle* was driving its popularity. The single continued to climb through June on all charts until it reached No. 1 in the week ending July 9, dislodging "Unchained Melody," a ballad from a nondescript film called *Unchained*. (Since the July 9 issue of *Billboard* came out on July 2, a Saturday, that's the day it officially ranked No. 1.)

It was during an early morning trip from New York to Boston in Haley's Cadillac that Marshall Lytle first realized what a hit they had. "[The car had] one of those new radios where you pushed a button and it went to the next station. I turned on the radio and hit the button and the station was playing 'Rock Around the Clock.' I hit the button again and the next station was play-

The 1955 reissue of "Rock Around the Clock," sparked by the release of Blackboard Jungle, *retained Decca's 1954 catalog number, but by now the company had changed the font, or script, of its logo.*

ing 'Rock Around the Clock,' and the next station, too. Within two minutes that morning, I heard 'Rock Around the Clock' play on twelve different stations simultaneously."

Aside from its presence in *Blackboard Jungle*, there were other reasons why people were ready to listen to "Rock Around the Clock." A lot had happened between its original release in May 1954 and its reappearance in April 1955. For one, rhythm and blues, a niche market only a couple of years earlier, had become the recording industry's biggest story. Consider, for example, that *Billboard*'s listing of "The Nation's Top Ten Tunes" for the week ending February 16, 1955, contained white cover records of five R&B songs. There were "Sincerely" by the McGuire Sisters at No. 2, "Hearts of Stone" by the Fontane Sisters at No. 3, "Ko Ko Mo" by Perry Como at No. 4, "Earth Angel" by

In 1955 the seven-inch 45-rpm single of "Rock Around the Clock" outsold its ten-inch 78-rpm counterpart several times over, signaling to the record industry that the aging, larger format was becoming a dinosaur.

the Crew-Cuts at No. 6, and "Tweedlee Dee" by Georgia Gibbs at No. 8. Furthermore, the original black recordings of these hits (by the Moonglows, the Charms, Gene & Eunice, the Penguins, and LaVern Baker, respectively) were also doing so well that *Billboard* added an R&B disc jockey chart.

Almost every week the trade magazines were running articles chronicling R&B's rags-to-riches popularity. In the March 26 *Billboard*, for example, Paul Ackerman, in a piece called "R&B Tunes' Boom Relegates Pop Field to Cover Activity," wrote that despite the industry's antagonism toward black music, "13 of the 30 disks on the current best-selling singles chart fall into that category." A few months later, in July, *Billboard* declared: "One of the more interesting talent developments of the last year has been the emergence of the Negro as a pop artist in the disk field. The trend is allied to the great expansion of rhythm and blues and the influence of that category on the pop music business."

It didn't hurt that pundits, preachers, civic leaders, and even black newspapers and disc jockeys were condemning many blue-tinted R&B songs, such as "Work With Me, Annie" and "Honey Love," as "smutty" and "obscene junk"—reproachful words guaranteed to send legions of teenagers scurrying into record shops to find out what all the fuss was about. Then, as R&B morphed into rock 'n' roll and exerted a greater pull on white record buyers, it took an even heavier pounding, especially from the nation's religious quarters, thanks, indirectly, to Senator Lyndon B. Johnson from Texas, who a year earlier, during a floor debate on the 1913 Internal Revenue Code, had added a provision preventing nonprofit organizations from participating in election campaigns. Johnson stated: "This amendment seeks to [deny] tax exempt status to not only those people who influence legislation but also those who intervene in any political campaign on behalf of any candidate for any public office" (100 Congressional Record, 59604, 1954). Denied the right to wage war on liberal politicians, tax-free busybodies were forced to redirect their Puritan outrage toward cultural surrogates. Juvenile delinquents and the degenerate stuff they read and listened to were a good start.

The previous April, only a week after the Comets recorded "Rock Around the Clock," a four-man Congressional Subcommittee to Investigate Juvenile Delinquency in the United States, led by Tennessee Senator Estes Kefauver, had begun public hearings in New York City to make a "full and complete study" of the "extent and character" of youthful malfeasance. The subcommittee's bible was New York psychiatrist Fredric Wertham's best-selling book, a nearly four-hundred-page screed blaming most of the young generation's dysfunction on "crime and horror comic books." According to Wertham, these comics "offer short courses in murder, mayhem, robbery, rape, cannibalism, carnage, necrophilia, sex, sadism, masochism, and virtually every other form of crime, degeneracy, bestiality, and horror." When E.C. Comics and other comic book publishers buckled under the pressure and toned down their content, the committee—along with its Jesus-juiced cheerleaders—turned next to the music industry that was peddling the aural equivalent of gory Crypt Keeper tales.

And just in time, because something had to be done. Young people, traditionally the main engine of the pop music market, were abandoning their parents' wholesome records and radio stations and listening to what polite critics were beginning to call "jungle music." "DJ Surveys Show Top Jocks May Not Be Best Pluggers," the February 25, 1955, *Billboard* announced. "According to the [Teen Age Survey Service], which recently polled deejay preferences of high school students in [the New York] area (generally conceded to be the biggest segment of pop buyers), the top 10 high school spinners here" included only four major radio personalities. The rest were broadcasting from smaller stations that played music out of the mainstream—rhythm and blues and, to a lesser extent, country music.

Most of the credit, or blame, for this turbulent turnabout could be laid at the studio door of Aldon James "Alan" Freed, the flamboyant, half-Jewish, Baptist-raised disc jockey from Salem, Ohio. In September 1954 Freed, age thirty-one, had moved his *Moondog House Party* from the boondocks of Cleveland to New York City, where he increased the ad revenues of his new station, WINS, by over forty percent within a few months. His show was also being syndicated to dozens of stations around the country. In November, when one of Manhattan's colorful street musicians, Louis Hardin—known around town as Moondog—got an injunction restraining WINS from using his moniker, Freed fell back on a line of patter he frequently used to describe his show—"A rock and roll session with rhythm and blues records!"—and retitled his nightly program the *Rock and Roll Party*. He cemented his new identity by incessantly repeating the phrase between records—and sometimes cutting in over them. For example, as he played his rousing new theme song, saxophonist Red Prysock's "Rock 'n' Roll," he'd shout above the fray, "Yeah, top twenty-five rock 'n' roll favorites, everybody, according to your mail requests, your telegrams, and your purchases all over the rock 'n' roll kingdom!" Two months later Freed sold out two "Rock and Roll Jubilee Balls" at the six-thousand-seat St. Nicholas Arena, where black artists played to a young, racially mixed audience. WINS daily hailed Alan Freed as "America's #1 Rock and Roll Disc Jockey." R&B record companies, angling for any advantage in the thriving new teen market, began touting their new releases in trade paper ads as "rock and roll"—using various conjunctive forms (either an 'n' or an ampersand, mostly). Finally, *Variety* put the official seal of approval on the term when one of its columnists, Herm Schoenfeld, referred to Freed as "the rock and roll disc jockey."

Much of this, it turned out, was the result of a calculated business deal between Freed and the man who brought him to New York, Morris Levy, who managed nightclubs and ran various shady music publishing and management companies for the Genovese mob. Seeing the marketing advantage of using rock 'n' roll as a euphemism to deracinate rhythm and blues, Levy copyrighted it. But Freed's constant flogging of the rock 'n' roll mantra as a part of his nightly shtick of thumping phone books, banging cowbells, and spinning the most raucous singles worked all too well. Rock 'n' roll became so popular and generic so quickly that even Morris Levy had to concede that his copyright was unenforceable. The term was part of the national lexicon by the time Decca reissued "Rock Around the Clock."

Decca executives discovered the growing teenage audience for rock 'n' roll as soon as reorders tumbled in from record distributors around the country. By now the 45-rpm single had gained parity with the venerable 78, so Decca's initial pressing for "Rock Around the Clock" had been roughly fifty-fifty. But the 45s were the ones flying off the shelves. Since older Americans were generally the ones still holding on to their 78 players, the explosion in 45 sales meant "Rock Around the Clock" was, to use a modern expression, "skewing young." Reorders for Decca's latest Kitty Kallen pop single remained dominantly 78s, but pressing plants had to start working their 45 stampers overtime to meet the demand for Bill Haley and His Comets. By June, *Cash Box* announced, "Bill Haley and his Comets, with Decca Records only 13 months, have hit a sales figure of over 3,000,000, according to diskery execs. 'Rock Around the Clock'…has gone over 1,000,000. Haley's 'Shake, Rattle, and Roll' hit a similar figure. His two other singles in the 13-month period, 'Dim, Dim the Lights' and 'Mambo Rock,' plus EP sets, raise the overall figure to 3,000,000." On June 29, *Variety* put "Rock Around the Clock" at the top of its "Retail Disk Best Seller" list.

But victory wasn't official until "Rock Around the Clock" reached the pinnacle of *Billboard*'s pop pyramid on July 2, 1955, four days before Bill Haley's thirtieth birthday. It was a strange and exotic interloper, considering that the other records rounding out the Top 5 were the typical orchestral ear candy of the day. And when "Rock Around the Clock" was finally unseated from its aerie nine weeks later, in early September, the usurper was Mitch Miller's snare-drum-driven "Yellow Rose of Texas," a Civil War–era minstrel song about a light-skinned mulatto girl—a "high yellow"—that Miller had transformed into an innocuous choral march for football halftimes. In such staid company, "Rock Around the Clock" sounded like something recorded on Mars.

The Comets had really hit the big time, and in the midfifties the big time

Even at the height of Comet mania, Bill Haley, seen here in a 1956 photo, always presented himself as a dignified musician instead of a rock 'n' roll wild man—an attitude that gradually diminished his popularity.

meant television. Jumping and jiving and rollicking on the stage, they became the first emissaries of rock 'n' roll, taking it right into the homes of tens of millions of Americans. They had already, on May 31, performed "Rock Around the Clock" on Milton Berle's NBC variety show, just as the record was starting to move. At roughly the same time, on ABC, Hollywood dancer Ray Bolger hired them to appear on his floundering *The Ray Bolger Show* in hopes of shoring up his ratings (to no avail; the show tanked in June). Then, two months later, on August 7, with their song at the top of the charts for the fifth week in a row, they appeared on Ed Sullivan's top-rated Sunday night CBS variety show, *The Toast of the Town* (soon to be renamed *The Ed Sullivan Show*). "Rock Around the Clock" also popped up on one of network TV's oddest programs in 1955, *The Dotty Mack Show*, which consisted of normal-looking people and slightly wacky-looking puppets pantomiming to the hits.

The Comets were attracting crowds everywhere they played, and since these new fans knew them only through their recordings, they wanted to hear those great Danny Cedrone and Art Ryerson solos. "We didn't have a lead guitar at that time," said Dick Richards. "Bill was more or less playing lead, but he was more like a country picker to the people hearing our records. When you added Billy Williamson playing steel, that just gave us too much of a country flavor." Fortunately, Haley had a thirty-three-year-old guitarist standing in the wings named Francis "Franny" Beecher, a Norristown resident whom Williamson had introduced to the Comets a year earlier. Beecher could play both country and jazz. More impressively, he knew every lick by the late Charlie Christian—the legendary black guitarist who'd indirectly had some influence on Cedrone—and he could play them well enough that Christian's mentor, bandleader Benny Goodman, had hired Beecher for a couple of years in the late forties. He'd already become the Comets' studio guitarist the previous September during the "Dim, Dim the Lights" session, and now, as the success of "Rock Around the Clock" demanded someone who could reasonably duplicate the famous solo, he became a full-time member of the stage band. Since his hollowbody Epiphone Emperor was more suited to jazz than to the high-volume antics of the Comets, the Gibson Guitar Company presented him with a promotional copy of its latest Les Paul solidbody electric guitar.

At Beecher's first shows with the Comets, the reaction of the young crowds shocked him. "The big bands like Goodman were very popular," he told David Hirschberg, "but they didn't produce the kind of hysteria we saw from the [Comets] fans—the screaming and the crying.... [We] were playing and some

Bill Haley's new Comets rode the international wave of "Rock Around the Clock." Left to right are saxophonist Rudy Pompilli, Billy Williamson, bassist Al Rex, Johnny Grande, drummer Ralph Jones, and guitarist Franny Beecher.

girls in the front row fainted. [The sax player] and I looked at each other and said, 'Can you believe that?'"

This hysteria began to spread beyond their shows. First came a harmless riot of sorts at Princeton University in New Jersey, where on a Tuesday night, May 17, 1955, according to the *Philadelphia Enquirer*, student dormitories began competing with each other by seeing who could play "Rock Around the Clock" the loudest, "making a mad medley which led to chanting and stamping by the staid Princetonians." Around midnight the students ran out of their dorms, set fire to a trash can, and paraded through the streets "until an assistant dean dampened their hilarity by pointing up the advantages of a more sedate mode of life."

Though rock 'n' roll became the media's favorite whipping boy, the most focused attacks came from within the music industry itself. In the early days, when the spinet was a common piece of furniture in the American parlor, the sales of sheet music transcriptions for voice and piano determined a song's popularity, and even by 1955 the sheet—with a photo of a popular artist or group on the cover—was still a fairly substantial segment of the market. But after "Rock Around the Clock," in the words of writer David Jasen, "[T]he list of each year's Top Ten songs would be almost entirely composed of rock and roll numbers which were not sold to any great extent in sheet music form. Popular music, which had been originally created for adults who went to vaudeville shows, theaters, nightclubs, and saloons, and who bought sheet music to sing and play, became dominated by teenagers who valued the performance more than the written music."

This new emphasis on the artist rather than the song was probably the most insidious change of all because it undermined what was left of the Great American Songbook that formed the bedrock of Tin Pan Alley. The best of this songbook were 32-bar nuggets, often called "standards," with internal rhymes and rhythms and exquisitely catchy melodies, carefully crafted by the likes of Irving Berlin, Cole Porter, Jerome Kern, Johnny Mercer, and George Gershwin. In the words of writer Jesse Green, they're classic songs that "trade in specific and complex emotions, expressed through a prism of artifice that bends them toward irony and abstraction." These standards were a boon to publishers because casual musicians bought the sheet music and professional artists reinterpreted them year after year.

On the other hand, "Rock Around the Clock" came from a folk tradition that "prizes authenticity above artifice and trades in large, generic feelings that are expressed as directly as possible." It also looked rather ridiculous on the printed page. That neither stopped Max Freedman's 1953 arrangement from being successful as sheet music, nor Jimmy Myers from commissioning a big band dance arrangement that was released as sheet music at the height of the single's popularity. But a song like "Rock Around the Clock" could be recorded really well only once. From then on, anyone who performed it was parroting or parodying the original.

Even worse, most early rock 'n' roll songs were owned by small publishing companies affiliated with Broadcast Music, Inc. (BMI), rather than with the American Society of Composers, Arrangers and Producers (ASCAP). (This was not the case, however, with "Rock Around the Clock," an ASCAP song.) The job of these two licensing agencies was to collect royalties whenever certain songs were played or performed in public, but ASCAP, Tin Pan Alley's 800-pound gorilla for the previous forty years, had also taken upon itself the duties of an industry lobbyist, restricting the most lucrative areas of the market—Broadway, Hollywood, the Big Three record companies—to its elite group of publishers and songwriters. But in recent years, ASCAP's exclusivity, especially its disdain of hillbilly and R&B music, had swelled the ranks of BMI, a smaller agency that radio network owners had started in the early 1940s to fend off ASCAP royalty hikes. The postwar rise of independent record companies and small publishers—not to mention radio's transformation from live entertainment to an on-air jukebox for records—was eroding ASCAP's influence. In 1953, out of desperation, it filed an unsuccessful $150 million anti-trust lawsuit against BMI, the three main radio networks, and two record companies, claiming they had colluded to keep ASCAP songs off the air. With the plummeting sales of sheet music making ASCAP publishers and songwriters more dependent on recordings for performance royalties at just the moment when the record industry was increasingly covering black and country songs, these professionals faced an uncertain future and were very unhappy about it. ("Rock 'n' roll is dull, ugly, amateurish, immature, trite, banal, and stale," hissed Meredith Willson, whose compositions included the less dull, less trite, less stale "Seventy-Six Trombones" and "Till There Was You" from the Broadway musical *The Music Man*.)

ASCAP's criticism, generally leveled by its surrogates at music magazines and trade publications, became so intense, and so personal, that by September 1955 Bob Thiele at Coral Records struck back publicly in *Cash Box*, defending his choice of BMI material for his artists, who included Teresa Brewer and the McGuire Sisters. A&R (artists and repertoire) men, said Thiele, "are under pressure [by management] to produce a salable record—one that the consumer wants," and judging from Coral's recent cover hits of R&B songs like "Sincerely" and "Pledging My Love," he had made the right choice. Besides, "covering means servicing a wider geographical spread of publishers," which gave A&R men a greater variety of music to choose from.

This was not what song publishers on Broadway wanted to hear. But all they could do for now, besides opening up their ranks to promising new songwriters, was use their influence within the music industry to bully and discredit rock 'n' roll by disparaging its stupid or dirty lyrics ("leer-ics," as *Variety* called them) and accuse disc jockeys of having a proprietary interest in some of the records they were spinning—in other words, accepting bribes, called "payola," in return for airtime. Why else would any radio station play mindless BMI junk?

An example of the steady drumbeat against rock 'n' roll was an interview in *Down Beat* magazine with Billy Taylor, the house pianist at the famous Birdland jazz club a couple blocks north of Times Square. Taylor denounced rock 'n' roll as being "obviously gimmicked up with old boogie-woogie phrases, pseudo-Spanish rhythms, recurring triplets, etc., *ad nauseam*. The melodies

Were they jazz? Rhythm and blues? Rock 'n' roll? As late as May 1956, jazz bible Down Beat *was trying to classify what the Comets were playing. One thing was certain: They were popular enough to boost magazine sales.*

CHAPTER 11: Rock Around the Clock Again **139**

are repetitious and/or plagiarized.... Harmonically, a lot of it is incorrectly written and even worse than that, incorrectly played." Taylor was also loath to give rock 'n' roll credit for returning dance rhythms to music. "The kind of beat it 'brought back' would have been better discarded. Even in the wildest days of down-home blues, there was always a little more subtlety than present-day rhythm and blues has with its insistent accent on two and four or its shuffle rhythms.... Even legitimate blues singers like Joe Turner have suffered. He has to have a Bill Haley-type rhythm section behind him to sell, but of all people, Joe doesn't need someone to make him swing."

Meanwhile, in addition to all the external forces against them, the Comets were suffering internal problems. Playing steadily around the country, the band was bringing in roughly $10,000 a week. That was good money for a tour in 1955, when admission tickets were less than two dollars, other acts on the bill shared the receipts, and touring contracts standardized nightly earnings whether they were playing to 2,500 people at the Rainbow Rondeau in Salt Lake City or nine thousand screaming fans at Pittsburgh's Seagram Mosque. Adding to the Comets coffers were quarterly royalty checks from Decca—including one for $17,000—as "Rock Around the Clock" approached the two-million mark. This was all well and good, except for one thing: Haley, Grande, Williamson, and manager Lord Jim Ferguson were equal partners in the Comets enterprise, but D'Ambrosio, Lytle, Beecher, and Richards remained employees, pulling down a flat weekly salary, plus expenses. Such a disparity in fortunes was corrosive among men sharing the same stage and the same cars night after night. "I was making about $200–$225 a week at that time," D'Ambrosio told Lee Cotten. "So were Marshall and Dick.... [W]e didn't feel like we were being treated right. We'd go on all the promotions with the band; we came up with the arrangements for the band. We were a very active part of that band, not just sidemen." At one point, when Haley visited a Cadillac dealership in Chicago where the Comets' equipment truck was being repaired, he was so offended by the dismissive attitude of the sales manager that he capriciously pointed to the biggest, yellowest Cadillac Coupe de Ville in the middle of the showroom floor and pulled out a wad of cash to pay for it, just to show that he was rich enough to buy and sell the guy. Such extravagance grated on the hired hands.

"In September of '55 we went to Haley and asked for a raise," Dick Richards told David Hirschberg. "He turned us down. The same week he bought a brand new Cadillac. We saw right then that no matter how big he got, we wouldn't get a piece of it. We were just salaried employees." Actually, the man who turned them down was Ferguson, who figured nobody would quit the country's hottest band. In early October Lytle, Richards, and D'Ambrosio gave Haley two weeks' notice that they were leaving. According to D'Ambrosio, "Bill went out and hired new musicians to take our place. So, for the next two weeks, wherever we played, these three guys were sitting in the front row, watching whatever we did." After playing their last gig with the Comets at the Broadhurst Hotel in Philadelphia, they went to Capitol Records under the name the Jodimars (taken from their first names Joey, Dick, and Marshall) and recorded in the big-beat Comets style for the next two years. "We made more money in our first two weeks as the Jodimars than we did in a year as the Comets," said Richards. On the minus side, they never had a sizable hit, and they missed out on making movies and traveling all over the world.

Lytle's replacement was Al Rex, Haley's original bassist from the Saddlemen days. D'Ambrosio's spot was taken by a jazz saxophonist from Chester named Rudy Pompilli, formerly of the Ralph Marterie Orchestra that had covered "Crazy Man, Crazy" two years earlier. Pompilli suggested a jazz drummer, also from Chester, named Ralph Jones to take over Richards' chair, even though he'd never played rock 'n' roll before. Nobody noticed the changing of the guard. From then on, said Grande, "The fans knew the new guys as the original Comets." "There was a slightly different sound in the band," Richards added. "You get a different sax man and the sound is going to change. But only a musician would know that."

Late in the fall the Comets were touring with Hank Snow for a week when Elvis Presley, an upcoming country star from the *Louisiana Hayride* radio program in Shreveport, joined the show for one performance in Oklahoma City, on October 16, and met Bill Haley for the first time. (Three weeks earlier Presley had paid homage to him by opening his show at the Civic Auditorium in Kingsport, Tennessee, with "Rock Around the Clock," a song he never recorded.) The two met again a few days later while they were playing separate shows in Cleveland, Ohio. During this stopover, on the afternoon of October 20, they took part in what would become the world's first rock 'n' roll documentary—though it would never be released in either Haley's or Presley's lifetime.

The 16-mm film, tentatively christened *The Pied Piper of Cleveland: A Day in the Life of a Famous Disk Jockey,* purported to follow the doings of Bill Randle. Now that his crosstown rival, Alan Freed, had moved to New York,

A relatively unknown Elvis Presley (backstage with Haley at Brooklyn High School in Cleveland, Ohio) opened for the Comets in late 1955. Within a few months the youngster would be rock 'n' roll's undisputed king.

Randle was the only big dog in town. Part of the film contained a rock 'n' roll show staged at the assembly auditorium of a high school in the Cleveland suburb of Brooklyn. It starred Presley, the Comets, crooner Pat Boone, and a white vocal group called the Four Lads. Later in the evening the same four acts did a second show for the general public at St. Michael's Hall on Cleveland's East 100th Street, which was also partially filmed.

In November, just as the trade papers were announcing that RCA Victor had signed Elvis Presley away from Sun Records, Universal Pictures in Hollywood came onboard to expand Randle's project. Another concert was scheduled for November 26, this time in New York, starring Bill Haley, the Crew-Cuts, Johnnie Ray, LaVern Baker, Tony Bennett, and a dozen other acts. Suddenly the deal fell apart. The New York cinematographers' union shut down the production, Universal backed out, and Randle never completed his film.*

It didn't matter, as far as the Comets were concerned. The same week the concert was canceled, their booker, Jolly Joyce, contacted Haley on the road. "Bill, you and the guys are going to Hollywood. You're making a movie about 'Rock Around the Clock.'"

---

*The unedited negative—seventeen or eighteen cans' worth—would languish in Universal's vaults for the next thirty-seven years, filed under the name *A Day in the Life of a Famous DJ*, until a group of British investors came looking for it. Since Bill Randle still legally owned the film, he sold his rights in 1992 for well over a million dollars. The investors turned around and sold the film to PolyGram for a reported $2.2 million. In the dozen years since, there have been intermittent announcements that the film will be released any day now.

CHAPTER 12

HOLLYWOOD ROCK 'N' ROLL

As *Variety*, the *Hollywood Reporter*, and *Billboard* issued daily and weekly reports from the cultural front on the "teenage riots" at Comets concerts and *Blackboard Jungle* screenings, it dawned on one producer in Hollywood that rock 'n' roll was ripe for cinematic exploitation, as long as he could get his product out into the marketplace *next week*—or as close to next week as possible. He didn't understand any music after Glenn Miller, but he knew that kids loved this Bill Haley guy and were crazy about whatever crap his band was playing.

And so this producer called the Jolly Joyce Theatrical Agency in New York, took his fat, soggy cigar out of his mouth, and said, "This is Sam Katzman at Columbia Pictures in Hollywood, and I want to do a movie about 'Rock Around the Clock' with your boys." The two veteran hustlers cut the deal over the phone and wrapped up the loose ends over the next few days. The production was slated for early January. For better or worse, but mostly worse, Sam Katzman would make the world's first rock 'n' roll movie.

The fifty-four-year-old Katzman was the epitome of the Tinseltown schlockmeister, a veteran of "programmers," or "B movies," who more recently was specializing in drive-in movies aimed at Midwestern audiences. Katzman had cranked out over a hundred cheapies since 1932, the year the studios began running "double bills"—two movies together—to keep Depression-ravaged audiences from deserting their theaters across the country. The powerhouses like MGM and Paramount in those days provided the featured attractions (the

"A movies" with big stars) and contracted with poverty-row operations like Katzman's to supply a time-killer to fill out the bill. Naturally these films had to be made on restricted budgets, so a B-movie producer stayed within rigid genres, avoided complicated scenes that might require more than two or three camera setups, limited the number of takes regardless of botched lines and sloppy continuity, and usually kept their running time below seventy minutes. Katzman's oeuvre included westerns, several Bela Lugosi mad scientist flicks, a series of Jungle Jim and East Side Kids movies, and some slave girl epics (i.e., *Siren of Bagdad*). His flatly lit, flatly acted productions were such an anathema to real Hollywood talent that Columbia Studios mogul Harry Cohn, who signed him to a distribution deal in 1952, reportedly kept his contract actors in line with the threat, "If you don't behave yourself, I'll loan you out to Sam Katzman." One of the most sterling reviews a Katzman movie ever got was: "It could have been worse." But he took all the barbs in stride, boasting, "Every one of my films made money." Huntz Hall, who starred in the East Side Kids series, remembered that once, when the director fell behind his quota of shooting ten script pages a day, Katzman came on the set, tore five pages out of the script, and declared the film back on schedule. Since his movies were notoriously riddled with non-sequitur scenes and pointless dialogue, he probably figured nobody would notice anyway.

For the Comets, making *Rock Around the Clock* turned out to be another series of dates on their busy touring schedule. After rocking in the New Year, 1956, at the packed Michigan State Fairground Coliseum in Detroit, they took an early Sunday train to Chicago to catch that evening's Santa Fe Super Chief to the coast, arrived in Los Angeles' Union Station thirty-six hours later, and caught a limousine to Hollywood, where they checked into the Knickerbocker Hotel on Ivar Street, just north of Hollywood Boulevard. (Elvis Presley would stay there a few months later while making *Love Me Tender*.) The next morning, according to Haley's diary, they "reported to Columbia Pictures at 11:30. Ran over a few tunes, got wardrobe information, met director, make-up man etc. for pictures." Two days later, on Friday, January 6, 1956, they started filming.

Fred F. Sears, a former B-movie actor who had cut his teeth directing a dozen Durango Kid westerns several years earlier, shot *Rock Around the Clock* on several musty backlot sets in thirteen days, from a script that James B. Gordon and Robert E. Kent had knocked out in even less time. Within a month *Rock Around the Clock* was edited and ready for an advance screening for Columbia's executives. It premiered on March 14 in Washington, D.C.

Columbia Pictures' 1956 low-budget Rock Around the Clock, *the first rock 'n' roll movie, set the standard for Hollywood's shoddy treatment of rock music for the next several years.*

Once again, the Comets' "Rock Around the Clock" blared over the opening credits to get the audience's adrenaline pumping, but this time there was no *Blackboard Jungle* drama to keep it going. The plot, a hand-me-down from the early days of sound, was simply there to string musical interludes together and give teenagers time to roam the aisles or neck in the balcony without missing anything. They could look up at the screen at any moment and instantly comprehend where they were in the story. The screenwriters were most likely inspired by Twentieth Century Fox's 1942 romantic comedy, *Orchestra Wives*, starring the Glenn Miller Orchestra, whose stage performances in front of jitterbugging teenagers were showcased within a semi-documentary story about love and jealousy on the road. But *Rock Around the Clock*'s $300,000 budget (from which Haley and Alan Freed were each paid $20,000) did not allow for *Orchestra Wives*' name stars or big production numbers.

Clocking in at 77 minutes, *Rock Around the Clock* opens with small-time promoter Steve Hollis (played by 1940s big-band singer Johnny Johnston) getting fired somewhere in the South by an orchestra leader who blames him, not the band's Depression-era music, for the empty dance floor. Hollis retorts, "The only thing that's stayed up to date in this band of yours is your watch."

Driving back to New York with his wisecracking sidekick, Corny (Henry Slate), Hollis stops at a motel in a hick town called Strawberry Springs. Instead of going straight to bed, they fall in step with a throng of teenagers heading to the town hall to hear a combo of local yokels led by a plump tractor mechanic with a spit curl over his forehead. As we enter the building, Bill Haley and His Comets are playing their real-life latest hit, "See You Later, Alligator," which has been edited with repeating choruses into a four-minute romp. Though the camera doesn't capture the Comets' stage dynamics very well, it has a good time with the jitterbugging "teenagers"—who like adolescents in most 1950s films look like they're in their late twenties. Corny observes that he hasn't seen anything like this since a flea circus act got loose at the Roseland Ballroom. "[The music] isn't boogie, it isn't jive, and it isn't swing," Hollis mutters. "It's all three mixed together." A girl on the dance floor, hanging upside down in her partner's arms, informs him in one of the film's better lines, "It's rock 'n' roll, brother, and we're *rockin'* tonight!"

Then, as the Comets go into "Rock-A-Beatin' Boogie," the film's love interest, Lisa Johns (Lisa Gaye, the real-life sister of Debra Paget, soon to be Elvis Presley's squeeze in *Love Me Tender*), shows off her choreography on the dance floor and the other kids exchange what passes for hep jive. So far so good. But when the dancing's over and Hollis decides to take Bill, the band, and Lisa to New York and introduce them to a major promoter, the plot, as it were, kicks in. The promoter happens to be Hollis' ex-girlfriend Corrine (Alix Talton), who's anxious to scuttle his career in hopes he'll come crawling back to her. She books Haley to play a hoity-toity senior prom at an exclusive Connecticut girls' school where she's certain the "jive outfit" will be booed off the campus. But Corrine hasn't considered rock 'n' roll's irresistible appeal. The Comets, with Lisa's help, get all the debs and their stuffy boyfriends to dig it the most with a liberating "Razzle Dazzle."

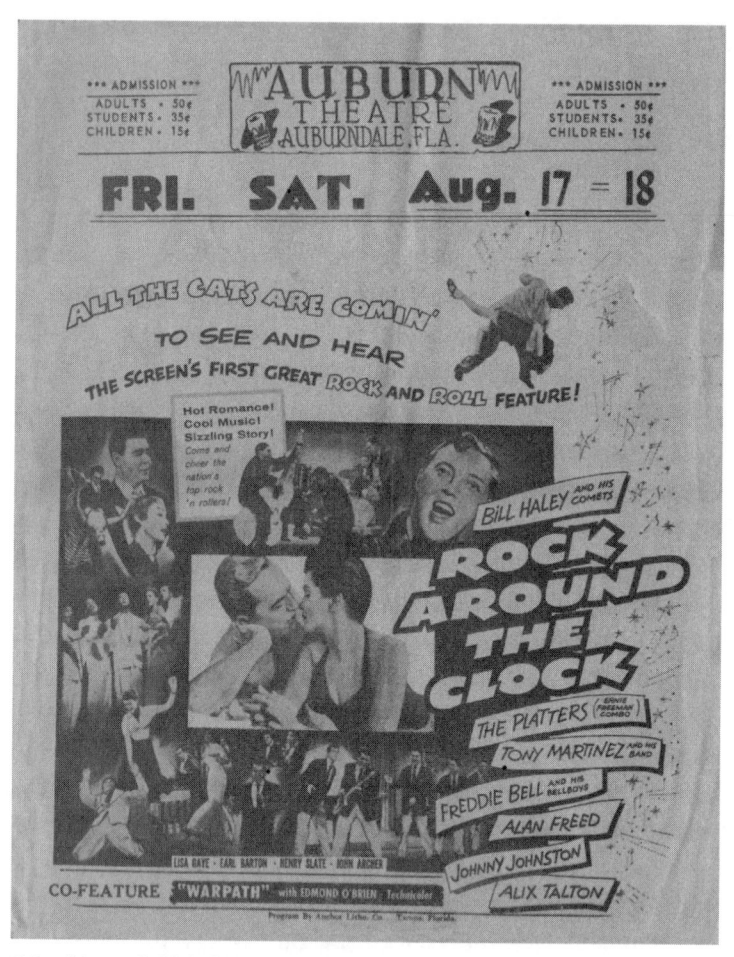

Columbia used old-fashioned ballyhoo and huckstering to sell Rock Around the Clock, a niche-market B movie. Thousands of pulpy flyers like this one for a small-town theater in Florida could be printed up cheaply.

Hollis hurries to the only person who can help him, Alan Freed, who without much arm-twisting agrees to take over the Comets' management. (Indicative of the haste in which the movie was made, the lighting director wasn't given time to mute the scars on Freed's face from a 1953 auto accident.) Next thing you know, the band's taking show biz by storm. With a fragment of "Rock Around the Clock" playing, we see a montage of the Comets romping onstage, a blazing club marquee, and a rave review from *Variety*.

Musically there are two high points to come. First, during a rehearsal at Freed's club, the Comets convincingly lip-sync to their newest single,

148 ROCK AROUND THE CLOCK

"R.O.C.K." Then, at a *Rock 'n' Roll Jamboree* TV show in Hollywood, they give a hint of their exciting stage show with an instrumental called "Rudy's Rock," a honking, acrobatic workout—the only song recorded live on Columbia's set—that lets saxophonist Rudy Pompilli and bass player Al Rex clown around the stage. And then, as the inconsequential story crumbles into a sudden, uninvolving denouement, "Rock Around the Clock" plays yet a third time—in truncated form—as the credits announce "The Living End."

For Comets fans, *Rock Around the Clock* was a feast of nine songs, including fragments of "A.B.C. Boogie" and "Happy Baby" (the Jimmy Myers B-sides of their second and third Decca singles) and "Mambo Rock." The Platters—a young, fifties update of the forties Ink Spots, with a girl added—sang their first two hits, "Only You" and "The Great Pretender." Also in the film were Freddie Bell and His Bellboys, a six-man lounge act from Philadelphia that played white R&B in the style of the Treniers. Leader Fred Bello sang "Giddy Up Ding Dong"—slang that went back to Louis Armstrong's 1931 recording of "I'm a Ding Dong Daddy"—and a heavy-footed "We're Gonna Teach You to Rock," both of which he'd scribbled out for Myers's publishing company as soon as he heard he was doing the movie. For the parents who might be chaperoning their kids to *Rock Around the Clock*, Tony Martinez and his Latin orchestra played a couple of mambo cha-chas. The Bellboys and Martinez were included in the film because their agent, Jolly Joyce, made them part of a package: If Katzman wanted the Comets, he'd have to take the others as well, a policy that afflicted most fifties rock 'n' roll films. (Incidentally, Freddie Bell and His Bellboys got their footnote in rock 'n' roll history three months later, after they returned to their residency at the Sands Hotel in Las Vegas. In April, while Elvis Presley was making his inauspicious Vegas debut at the Frontier Hotel to promote "Heartbreak Hotel," he went to see the Bellboys several times and took such a shine to the humorous way they had arranged and performed Big Mama Thornton's 1952 blues hit, "Hound Dog," that he did it Bellboy-style at his next recording session. "Hound Dog" became the biggest hit of 1956.)

At the end of February, after getting a sneak preview of *Rock Around the Clock* in Philadelphia, the Comets went on a promotional tour for the next couple of months as it opened around the country. Columbia's ballyhoo machine sent promotional booklets to theater owners, explaining how to create tie-ins with record stores, radio stations, and other businesses. "Get local ballrooms and dancing schools to use the [Comets'] records, with cooperative displays," was one suggestion. "List the [movie's] 17 songs in your ads and offer guest tickets to those who bring in records or sheet music of all" was another. To drum up excitement, local promoters needed to "arrange for disc jockeys to declare Bill Haley Week," to send sound trucks "rolling through the streets playing the recordings of Bill Haley and His Comets," and sponsor contests, such as the best letter explaining "Why I Want to See Bill Haley and His Comets in *Rock Around the Clock*." There was also merchandise that could be ordered, including a Rock Around the Clock record beanie "with the film's title stitched around the brim, and a removable, playable, 6-inch recording of the hit tune" on top, as well as Rock Around the Clock skirts and T-shirts adorned with a clock motif, dancing stick figures, and music notes. These items alone suggest that Columbia's flacks understood rock 'n' roll about as well as Katzman did.

Critics were generally kind to *Rock Around the Clock*, giving it faint praise that wasn't too damning. According to the *Los Angeles Times*, "the rhythm comes out on top. Some clever lines and fast paced plot...doesn't intrude too much on the music." The *Hollywood Reporter* "found this off-beat, low budget, black and white musical thoroughly entertaining." *Variety* said it "speaks the teenager idiom and will prove a handy entry for exhibitors picking a show

A Mexican lobby poster for Rock Around the Clock *featured disc jockey Alan Freed flanked by his costars Johnny Johnston and Lisa Gaye (the sister of Elvis Presley's love interest, Debra Paget, in* Love Me Tender*).*

aimed at the sweater-levi trade." *Film Daily* called it "a cut above many of the items [Katzman] turns out for the B-picture market...and Fred F. Sears has handled the directorial assignment competently." The *Los Angeles Examiner* pronounced it a good film for the "hepcats."

"See You Later, Alligator" turned out to be the film's only accompanying hit. The single had entered the Top 40 on January 14, 1956, a couple of days before Katzman finished principal shooting, and spent five months on the charts, reaching as high as No. 6. It was the perfect song for Haley, cleverly using a hip expression in the chorus—"see you later, alligator, after a while, crocodile"—that became a standard parting line among teenagers that year and eventually entered the national idiom. The song was a cover of a recent single on Chess Records called "Later, Alligator" by a seventeen-year-old Louisiana Cajun named Bobby Charles (*né* Guidry), who had lifted the chorus from "Later for You Baby," a 1954 record by Mississippi bluesman Guitar Slim. As soon as Bill Haley's Decca version hit the airwaves, Chess reissued Charles's recording as "See You Later, Alligator" and convinced their young singer to wear a spit curl over his forehead like Haley. Many rockabilly singers adopted Elvis Presley's sideburns and pompadour, but Charles was Haley's only tonsorial imitator.

(Incidentally, the term alligator in this context was a back-formation from 1920s black jive. A guy who was "with it" was called a "gate," or "gates," an allusion to a gate swinging back and forth, as in Louis Armstrong's line from his 1931 hit, "When It's Sleepytime Down South," when he asks a friend, "Whatcha say, Gates?" Or take Louis Jordan's lyrics from the 1940 song, "June Tenth Jamboree!": "Come on, Gates, and jump with me.... All the gates was having a ball." Lionel Hampton so commonly called everyone "Gates" that it became his nickname. Before long, good dancers and hepcats were "gaters," as in Cab Calloway's 1939 hit, "(Hep-Hep!) The Jumpin' Jive," in which he sang, "Make the joint jump like the gaters do." It was only a matter of time before the spelling changed. R&B sax man Willis Jackson's 1949 instrumental, "Gator Tail," and its follow-up, "Later for the Gator," were so popular that he became known as Gatortail Jackson, but his 1952 recording of "Gater's Groove" spelled out exactly where the term originated.)

If "See You Later, Alligator" was dead-on, "R.O.C.K."—the song Haley had banked on being *Rock Around the Clock*'s beneficiary—was nearly dead on arrival. Though "R.O.C.K." was recorded three months before "See You Later, Alligator," Milt Gabler hadn't deemed it release-worthy until Haley gave it a prominent place in the film. "R.O.C.K." entered the charts in late March and got a boost to No. 16 a couple of weeks later as *Rock Around the Clock* opened around the country. A self-referential recap of rock 'n' roll's beginnings, "R.O.C.K." wasn't a bad song, but there was nothing catchy about it, except a syncopated spelling gimmick borrowed from Johnnie Lee Willis's 1950 hit, "Rag Mop." The only thing recommending it as the soundtrack single was that Haley wrote it and owned the publishing. Its B side was "The Saints Rock 'n' Roll," an update of the traditional "When the Saints Go Marching In," whose arrangement he and Gabler had copyrighted. Haley's growing insistence on recording unspectacular songs simply because he owned them would from then on diminish his recording career. When "R.O.C.K." plummeted off the charts, he would never return to America's Top 20 again.

Bill Haley played a Gibson Super 400, and his studio guitarist, Danny Cedrone, played a Gibson ES-300. After "Rock Around the Clock," the Gibson company began supplying the Comets with free guitars.

Like *Blackboard Jungle*, *Rock Around the Clock* benefited from press accounts of mayhem in the balconies. *Variety* reported in April that the film "has run headlong into a storm of trouble which the offbeat music has stirred in several communities." Many of those towns and cities "have already taken legal steps to halt teenage hops and other gatherings at which rock 'n' roll is featured. In this connection, it's known that theater men have received warnings from local police, community groups, newspapers, etc. In some cases, exhib[itor]s are being told they are free to play the picture—but can use no campaign stunts which might set off trouble among the cultists."

Most of this tempest was Columbia Pictures hype designed to generate the kind of hysteria that got everyone talking about *Blackboard Jungle* the year before, and it worked. *Rock Around the Clock* eventually grossed four million dollars, twice what Columbia Pictures had expected. The Bellboys' Fred Bello later told British writer Spencer Leigh, "We never expected it to be that big, but it took off around the world. It took me to the Far East, South America—everywhere. And the Platters, myself, and Bill Haley toured for three or four years on the strength of it."

Three guys not happy with all this success were ex-Comets Joey D'Ambrosio, Marshall Lytle, and Dick Richards. D'Ambrosio and Lytle had been present on half the songs on the soundtrack. They were never paid a cent for their contributions. Worse, they had to watch other musicians pantomiming to their music. As Johnny Grande told Lee Cotten, "With the movie being so big, everyone thought Rudy Pompilli, Ralph Jones, and Al Rex were the originals."

As soon as *Rock Around the Clock* started packing kids into theaters, Sam Katzman ordered his screenwriters to bang out a sequel based on the criticism rock 'n' roll was getting from the media. A week later they brought him *Don't Knock the Rock!*, a tale of small-town authorities fighting off a rock 'n' roll invasion as if it had descended from outer space, until Bill Haley rode in to assure everyone that their kids were safe. (It's no surprise that Katzman's second-biggest film in 1956 was *Earth Vs. the Flying Saucers*.) This theme would be repeated in a dozen movies over the next several years, until a Philadelphia-born director named Richard Lester gave it a good whacking in a surreal British comedy called *It's Trad, Dad!* in 1962.

For *Don't Knock the Rock!* Katzman upped the budget to $500,000, though you wouldn't know it from watching the movie. The Comets performed only six mostly nondescript songs, with "Rip It Up" being the sole Top 40 visitor—though it was already long gone from the charts by the time the film came out.

Columbia Pictures was so surprised by Rock Around the Clock's *huge international grosses that it starred Bill Haley—along with Little Richard (above) and the Treniers—in a 1957 sequel called* Don't Knock the Rock.

Along for support were Little Richard (whose original version of "Rip It Up" had been a big hit earlier in the year) and the Treniers, the energetic R&B combo that should have been in *Rock Around the Clock* instead of the Bellboys. The role of the local "teenage rock singer" spearheading the town's music revolution was an uninspiring twenty-eight-year-old Italian crooner named Alan Dale (*né* Sigismondi), whose only hit had been a vocal cover of Perez Prado's "Cherry Pink (And Apple Blossom White)," the rococo trumpet rumba that "Rock Around the Clock" had replaced at No. 1 in 1955.

Released in late 1956, *Don't Knock the Rock!* made a profit but fell far short of *Rock Around the Clock*'s receipts. The *L.A. Times* was in accord with most publications when it called the film "a few gags and some drama, squeezed with no little effort into a series of rock and roll numbers." *Cue* magazine sardonically deemed it "not of Academy Award stature." The director, Fred Sears, celebrated its release with a fatal heart attack, and Sam Katzman, seeing that music fads were the answer, blissfully moved on to such masterpieces as *Cha Cha Cha Boom* and *Calypso Heatwave*. A few years later he would recycle the scripts of *Rock Around the Clock* and *Don't Knock the Rock!* to make *Twist Around the Clock* (1961) and *Don't Knock the Twist!* (1962), with Chubby Checker standing in for Bill Haley. Then he went on to produce a couple of Elvis Presley's worst movies, including *Harum Scarum*, in which Elvis saved Arabian dancing maidens in distress while singing "Shake the Tambourine."

All in all, *Rock Around the Clock* set a low standard for Hollywood's treatment of rock 'n' roll. Most of the films that followed were black-and-white bargain-basement jobs produced by middle-aged men who couldn't grasp the young market they were exploiting. The art direction and filmmaking styles were at least a decade behind the music. Whatever restless behavior these movies incited in the dark probably came from butt-aching boredom, because even fifties teenagers were savvy enough to know that the plots were creaking, clumsy, enervated banality, and the musical numbers, lacking any kaleidoscopic Busby Berkeley magic, had no kinetic energy. Outside of Elvis Presley's better films (*Loving You*, *Jailhouse Rock* and *King Creole*) and Twentieth Century Fox's *The Girl Can't Help It*—a spoof of the music industry, starring Jayne Mansfield's cantilevered boobs—there wasn't an A or even an A-minus movie among them.

Like his character in *Don't Knock the Rock!*, Bill Haley became the ambassador and elder statesman of rock 'n' roll, ready to challenge detractors and put it into historical and social perspective. "What I play and what I developed is a combination of Dixie, country and western, rhythm and blues, and pop," he told *Down Beat* in 1956, when the jazz magazine made him its cover boy. "[T]here was a void in music and people were looking for something with a simple beat." He pleaded rock 'n' roll's case to parents: "At the time that the kids are out listening to music, they're not getting into trouble. When they're home listening to records, they're not getting into mischief. It can only help them, not hurt them." He admonished other musicians for complaining about rock 'n' roll instead of capitalizing on it. "At the moment, big bands are unprofitable, but there is no reason why the ballroom operators and musicians can't convert to rock 'n' roll, because I know for a fact that a lot of the musicians who think that my music is bad are not working steadily." And he fended off charges of indecency. "I have always been careful not to use suggestive lyrics. Usually I try to use expressions that the kids can easily remember and repeat." In short, Bill Haley was beginning to talk down to his audience.

But as media criticism of rock 'n' roll in general and his own music in particular became more scathing, his old insecurities began gnawing at him. He developed a fear of his own fans. Reporters unnerved him. He started carrying

Though nominally the star of Don't Knock the Rock, *Bill Haley (with sax man Rudy Pompilli, drummer Ralph Jones, guitarist Franny Beecher, and steel guitarist Billy Williamson) was already out of favor with teenagers.*

a gun on tour. Increasingly he longed for the privacy, comfort, and safety of the compound, Melody Manor, he'd built for himself and his family in Booth's Corner.

Perhaps he sensed his fate. Going up against Dean Martin, Perry Como, and Eddie Fisher in 1954–55 was one thing, but when the much younger, better-looking Presley arrived fully formed in early 1956, Haley's days on top were over. He was too old for the teenage market. His music lacked the intimacy and emotional commitment that tugged the heartstrings of young girls and taught them the ABCs of love. His persona had no swaggering cool, no sexual danger, no tortured religious darkness, no iconic symbols—pink Cadillacs, blue suede shoes, turned-up collar, duck's-ass hair style—to make the boys want to emulate him. By the end of that first full-on year of the rock 'n' roll craze, its first star would be its first has-been, at least in America.

But new frontiers lay elsewhere. "Rock Around the Clock" was a hit all over the world. On New Year's Day, 1957, the Comets flew to Australia, their first stop on what would be rock 'n' roll's first world tour over the next two years.

CHAPTER 13

HELLBOUND TRAIN TO WATERLOO

(A British Remembrance by Former Pop Star Ian Whitcomb)

Young and restless England, stirred up by rough sounds from gramophones and fairground loudspeakers, was waiting for Bill Haley to come and take the war-weary country by storm, to shake it out of the doldrums and into the modern world. The local crooners in cardigans, with pipe and slippers at hand, moaning since the 1930s in mid-Atlantic accents, had better retreat home to their maisonettes. The liberating Yanks were coming!

So it was that Bill Haley and his Merry Men, supported by wives, arrived by boat and took the train to London. Mobs cheered them to the heavens, causing soot to fall and ancient music halls to lose heavy plaster. Hucksters sold Haley's hotel bathwater as if it were a holy relic. His "Rock Around the Clock," having already soared twice to great heights in England, returned to the charts yet a third time—and not the last.

Bill Haley. What a comfortable, homespun name! Fond as I was of him, I imagined the cheerful rustic in a nightcap, with a mug of hot chocolate at his bedside. As opposed to *Elvis Presley*, a sultry Greek god from a *Classics Illustrated* comic, who was never happy in bed unless there were kicks going on there. Both were revered and taken seriously in England, much more so than in their homeland of endless turnover. America may fashion heroes, but it's we British who preserve them.

Ours was a protected world, a cozy corner. True, we suffered privations—candy rationing, sausages stuffed with bread, ice cream made from margarine, shapeless clothes of rough material—but the young know of nothing else, so that while we were still cramped under World War II conditions, it all seemed perfectly normal. All in all, we youngsters lived comfortably—at least those of us in the leafy South of England, where history and culture seeped from old walls down country lanes lined with medieval hedges. Charming, but also cold and confining.

The rest of the world consisted of a quilt of colored shapes stamped on the revolving tin globe that took pride of place in the main classroom of my boarding school. Much of that globe was red, which meant we owned it and there was still a British Empire somewhere under the sun. On this same globe, if you revolved it to the far side, across a vast expanse of blue, could be found a great slab of a continent, the source of all that was un-English, all that was in full color and full of noise.

While I ought to have been studying the Wars of the Roses, I was actually studying about this faraway paradise. My sources, hidden under desktops and dormitory blankets, were *The Western Film Annual*, *Top Record Stars* (hardback), and then the scruffy paper inkies like *New Musical Express* and *Melody Maker*. My hands were black after touching them but my rapture was complete. There, in America, was an industry working night and day to crank out amazing sights and sounds, a clanking carousel expelling non-stop excitement. It was a boy's world run by adults who created cowboys, gangsters, crooners, tight jeans, ten-gallon hats, snap-brim fedoras—everything considered tasteless and vulgar in England.

"You're over-excited and making too much noise," my history master told me one day. "You laugh and sing all the time—and, what's worse, you lead the other boys in laughter and song. You must learn to take your place in proper society. Report to the headmaster for punishment!"

Fortunately, there was another commanding figure in my life to counter the masters of joylessness: Bill Haley, chief of his very own Comets. They were pictured as big, broad, genial bruisers in jackets that spelled *circus*—tuxedos in plaid—aided by a whiff of western outlawry. Yet their sunny smiles suggested they could be related to Hopalong Cassidy and his saddle pals, heroes of the six p.m. children's hour on BBC television. I liberated Haley and His Comets from an inkie and taped them lovingly to the front of my modern History Assignment binder, as if it were my passport out of old-time Britain.

Pictures are potent, but it was the music that had hit me first. I'll never forget that night in the dormitory when my huge hissing radio finally made proper contact with Radio Luxembourg, the only station brave enough to play the new music, from out over the English Channel, in the Grand Duchy. Suddenly there came roaring the sound of a great honking train, clickety-clacking across the sky, firing off rim shots at gray music teachers cowering below and dropping molten rock on the history-laden trees. A care package from America. A disc called "Rock Around the Clock."

There was another "Rock Around the Clock," though, and it was sinister and sexy, conveyed from a cinema screen. Over the school holidays during the Easter of 1955, I slinked up to the West End of London to catch a film whose reputation had preceded it in a vast wash of ink: *Blackboard Jungle* is part of a "new cycle of violent Hollywood movies," warned my weekly *Picturegoer* magazine. "There's *Black Tuesday* and *The Desperate Hours*, spreading the disease of the Big City and enticing youngsters to catch the fever," lectured the editors. "And now, picturegoers, there's this slice of reality"—a topical story of thuggery in the classroom, far from *Tom Brown's Schooldays*, containing an "icy, terrifyingly tense knife fight scene between master and pupil that has had British picturegoers tingling on the edge of their seats!" And worse, for after the lights went up and "God Save the Queen" was played, customers pushed and shoved their way out of the cinema.

In the darkness I was thrilled to the bone from the first moment, for there, slap up against the opening credits, was the march-to-arms anthem I'd heard under the dorm bedclothes. Only now it was militant in documentary black and white. We'd received our orders and they were set in the asphalt of a grim schoolyard enclosed by a concentration camp fence. The avuncular Haley of radio, disc, and photo had now, by association, become the voice of rebellion.

Then, of course, there followed the satisfying scene in which the juvies smash up the prized jazz record collection of teacher Richard Kylie. Satisfying for me because my school peers had been nagging me with their cant of jazz and how Haley didn't swing. Their kind of swing sounded like stodgy indolence to my ears, warmed-over leftovers from the days when big bands ruled, epochs ago. No, no, they countered: jazz was modern, progressive, intellectual, sophisticated—*de rigueur* for someone of my upper-middle-class stature.

Emerging from the cinema in a state of high excitement, and needing a dose of Haley, I raced into the nearest record store: Dobell's Jazz Record Shop. I should have known better. I was deep in enemy territory. The men who staffed Dobell's knew their music, but it stopped at jazz—modern jazz at that. They were famous for their password challenges such as Getz, Coltrane, and Monk. Trembling and pink, I dared to say Haley and was promptly given the freeze. The clerks returned to their discussion on the use of parallel fifths in riffing. I beat a hasty retreat.

Also here in the West End, in Soho, away from the bomb craters and ruined churches, clustered the trading posts of American culture. Record shops, movie distributors, hamburger cafes reeking of fried onion, and strip clubs. Round the corner and into Oxford Street I hurried because I knew that there, at the HMV record shop, I could obtain the new Bill Haley LP.

The cover had a red background and on top was simply the word ROCK with each letter designed as a trinket on a charm bracelet. It wasn't very stirring or revolutionary. And where was Bill's picture? Not attractive enough?

Great Britain's top pop music magazine, New Musical Express, *greeted Bill Haley and His Comets with a royal welcome when they arrived in 1957 to tour the country promoting the film* Rock Around the Clock.

160 ROCK AROUND THE CLOCK

Still, Bill's name was in good solid company there in the grand HMV record shop, stacked up amidst Frank Sinatra and Peggy Lee. He was legitimate, enshrined in vinyl and sheathed in shiny lamination. The liner notes informed me that Bill, as a poor lad, had been "forced to manufacture his own guitar out of cardboard." After that he'd yodeled with a traveling medicine show. More to the point, and ominously, the writer told us: "Let it rock—this is hard-driving stuff not for babies and grandmothers, tough music for a tough generation."

I took the Underground home to Wimbledon; all was well until I changed at Earl's Court. Suddenly a bellowing chant grew nearer and my fellow passengers pressed themselves against the station walls. Down the tube platform I saw marching towards me in uneven ranks a mass of costumed youths, flaying their arms out and reciting their war chant: "One, two, three o'clock, four o'clock *fuck*! We're gonna fuck around the clock tonight!" This monstrous army was made up of Teddy Boys and their ilk.

At one time you hardly ever saw these troublesome "common boys" because they had no money to seek public amusement. They had no cars, no motorbikes. They were literally working-class, spending their days slaving in factories or down the mine. They wore flat caps and rough suits. They kept quiet and knew their place. Occasionally I'd see them out on Wimbledon Common with their slingshots and sticks, attacking small animals. Yet I rather envied these yobs. There was a primitive masculinity about them that made me feel effete, as if I'd missed out on nature's adventure and needed the jungle experience.

But by 1955 they had money and decent jobs. They were becoming a force to be reckoned with. They had no interest in soccer, rugby, or cricket. No interest in the arts—not even in music. Dance halls were for poofs. The streets of London were where these boys hung out, beyond traditional British society.

And yet, sartorially, they displayed a sense of the past. Proud as peacocks, parody descendants of the "macaronis" of the eighteenth century, the Teddy Boys more directly derived their name from Edwardian dandies with their costume of drape jacket with velvet lapel, brocade waistcoat, drainpipe tight trousers. But elegance was spoiled by the Teds' fondness for the riverboat gambler's bootlace-thin tie, suede shoes with thick crepe soles (termed "brothel creepers"), fluorescent socks, and a nasty habit of filling their voluminous jackets with bicycle chains, flick knives, and other primitive weaponry. Their hair was long and greased and piled up into a quiff called a "back sweep and crest," so that a decent Ted resembled an angry cockerel. Due to the cruel wind and rain of London, his elaborate coiffure had to be constantly kept in place by skilled manipulation of a metal comb. To see a Ted arrange his hair with one swift swoop was to see urban folk art in action. Or so we were told by bold journalists, who also noted that Teds eschewed a traditional romantic interest in girls. They didn't take their lady to tea, or to a dance. Girls were "slags" or "birds" whose sole function was to service them—as in the command: "Clap your laughing gear round the end of my fuck stick, dearie!"

In 1954 the first Best-Dressed Ted Contest was held at Canvey Island, Essex. The papers also reported a gruesome murder on Clapham Common by a Teddy gang. Youth crimes had shot up by fifty percent. There were more boys than girls, a result of wartime birth bias, and any society fears an over-supply of unattached and restless young males. Proper Britain, still run by the upper classes under a set of rules and regulations based on good manners, was alarmed.

So there was I on the tube station platform with an army of Teds heading my way as they chanted a foul version of "Rock Around the Clock." What did I do? I moved out of their way and caught the next train home. Safe at last, I enjoyed a supper of sausages and baked beans followed by Queen's pudding, sitting at the bridge table as we all watched the TV news, read by a plummy-voiced gentleman in a dinner jacket and black bow tie. Afterward, I went to my room and played the Bill Haley LP—every lovely rolling track, every number steaming into one continuous railroad rhythm.

A few months later the Teds would discover their lodestone in the inside of a picture palace. *Rock Around the Clock* came to Britain in 1956 and, oddly enough, played without incident in three hundred cinemas. But when it came to South London, the signal went out that here was the mecca to make for, here was where the true purpose of rock 'n' roll could be expressed. Bill Haley was up on the screen, smiling and swaying and selling his homemade brew, but in the auditorium nobody was paying any attention. The lads, having slashed their seats, got up to jive in the aisles with each other, watched by their birds. Tuxedoed managers remonstrated, only to be doused by fire extinguishers. Pigeons were let loose and rockets set off, chewing gum was ground into the carpet by winklepickers, but worst of all, Bill's face up on the screen was pelted with ice cream and other refreshments. Rock youth had found its clubroom.

After the movie they spewed out into the streets. The papers reported traffic held up on Tower Bridge by dancing teenagers, policemen being kicked, cups and saucers thrown about, a mob in Lewisham chanting "Nine Little Policemen Hanging on the Wall." One-pound fines were handed down. The King of the Teddy Boys was jailed for "insulting behavior." The *Evening News* critic was baffled by the film and went in search of a double brandy. *The Daily Worker*, a communist paper, found the film direct and refreshing: "The music isn't obscene but the relentless commercialism is." Members of the House of Lords called for its banishment, and Lord Boothby claimed it threatened "the shell of civilization." The Queen, in the swim of things as usual, had a print of *Rock Around the Clock* sent up to Balmoral Castle, her Scottish retreat, by fast train. Her verdict was not recorded, but before long society columnists reported that she and her husband, the Duke of Edinburgh, were rocking and rolling till two A.M. at the Duke of Kent's twenty-first birthday party.

Then the December 22, 1956, edition of *The Record Mirror*, one of several British pop inkies, announced, "Rumours are strong that [the Comets] will soon be visiting us. Let's hope so—bands like this need to catch the wave as soon as possible in this crazy business. Who knows? The next craze could be the Mambo!"

Over in Pennsylvania, USA, as I would later learn, King Bill was relaxing at his custom-built home, Melody Manor. The estate held the past in remembrance and reverence: Bill's childhood house lay on the grounds next to the schoolhouse where he had studied and yodeled; fronting the long brick Manor itself was a shack boasting a flurry of chickens. He had built the house for his British-born mother, but she had died before it was ready. There swiftly followed the deaths of his father, sister, and his baby child. Despite the great financial success it brought him, 1956 was a horrid year. Bill was determined to protect and cherish his remaining family, his new wife, Cuppy, and the rest of their children.

The Manor, thus, was a sanctuary. Bill loved being surrounded by likeminded folks. Call them a retinue, an entourage, a gang of hangers-on. Some probably were friends. When Bill threw parties, one might find his manager, Lord Jim Ferguson, holding forth in the den, his legendary belly pressing against the bar, scotch in one hand and cigar in the other. Behind him his booker, Jolly Joyce, might be teaching the band boys how to play pool. In the kitchen Cuppy struggled to put together Bill's favorite dish, Lancashire Hot Pot, from one of his mother's treasured recipes. The children were somewhere safe—probably chasing around the maze of paths Bill had landscaped throughout his many wooded acres. With the new extended family taking the

British Brunswick Records put Bill Haley on the cover of one of its record-listing supplements in early 1957. Haley was always treated with greater respect in Great Britain than in his home country.

place of the recently deceased blood relatives, Christmas 1956 turned out to be the best one they'd ever had, what with Cadillacs glistening in the snow and contented hens cackling in the coop.

The outside world was forbidden entry into Melody Manor, because Bill was a very private person, still that shy boy of his childhood, wary of strangers. He didn't care much for traveling, especially by air, and hated having his photograph taken when he wasn't looking. With only one eye, he was never sure what side they were coming from. But the siren call soon came from across the sea, beckoning Bill to leave his safe haven.

In early January Lew and Leslie Grade, bigwigs in British showbiz, with experience dating back to the Charleston contests of the 1920s, were pleased to announce, in conjunction with the Rank Organization chain of cinemas, a three-week tour by Bill Haley and His Comets, commencing on February 7 at the Dominion Theatre, Tottenham Court Road, London. Two shows a night plus a fully supporting program of selected acts. Tickets sold out almost immediately. Bill issued a statement: "While the United States of America is my native land, England is my mother's land. She was born in Ulverston, in North Lancashire. I owe America a loyal citizen's allegiance. I owe England a deep affection."

What he didn't know was that somebody in his entourage had done a deal with *The Daily Mirror*, Britain's best-selling tabloid, for a series of columns written by Bill but in fact ghosted by staffer Noel Whitcomb (no relation). The journalist, an older man known for his natty Trilby and tips on horse racing, had Bill soft-soaping the locals with lines like: "I'm sorry about that commotion (referring to the *Rock Around the Clock* movie riots). I'm sorry about the disturbances and any trouble that followed." How did that go down among the Teds and Rockers?

Never before had an American rock 'n' roller played Britain and so, for a while, Bill's (I mean Whitcomb's) mollification was let by. "We can show the youngsters that fun can be clean.... Rock 'n' roll has a respectable musical background," and so on. Meanwhile, the real Bill had been persuaded to test his touring mettle prior to the British dates with a visit to Australia. Whoever organized the shows knew his stuff: Bill was the star of a genuine rock 'n' roll package—the supporting acts included Freddie Bell & His Bellboys and the Platters (his co-stars in *Rock Around the Clock*), as well as Jolly Joyce's newest client, the old Boss of the Blues himself, Big Joe Turner, whose "Shake, Rattle, and Roll" had been Bill Haley's first major hit. The tour was a financial triumph, they played in packed stadiums, but Bill usually locked himself in his hotel room, drinking coffee and other beverages, and making laconic entries in his diary: "Visited aboriginal village. Met champion boomerang thrower."

Two days after he'd returned from Australia to Melody Manor, he was off to England. Boarding the *Queen Elizabeth* luxury liner on January 31, 1957, were no less than seventeen members of the Haley party. Besides the Comets there were the reluctant Cuppy, Jolly Joyce, roadie "Catfish" Vince, and Lord Jim and his seventy-seven-year-old mother. Also on board was Bill's ghost writer, Noel Whitcomb, with his Trilby and cigarette holder, already installed in a huge stateroom where he sent Haley statements back to *Daily Mirror* readers: "We're rockin' through the ocean and rollin' through the waves keeping our telescopes at the ready to dig that crazy train at Southampton."

In fact, Bill had a dreadful voyage. They hit stormy weather, including a hurricane. "Can't wait till we get off this blooming boat," he wrote in his diary. They disembarked at Southampton on the afternoon of Tuesday, February 5. Bill was shaken silly by the sound of the ship's horn. Only it wasn't the horn. It was the regimented cry of a host of fans on the dock: "HALEY!!!"

All hell, it seemed, had been let loose. A hell of sloshed mud and pelting rain, watched by indignant residents from the windows of Edwardian hotels where palm court music still held sway. Five thousand fans, counted the newspaper men. What a story! "5,000 people almost killed us," Bill wrote in his diary. Hundreds of them had traveled down from London's Waterloo station on the Rock 'n' Roll Special, organized by *The Daily Mirror*. Bill had no idea he was to travel to London with this rabble, but he smiled while trying to assess the situation with his good eye. He and Cuppy were imprisoned in the car sent to convey them to the railway station. Fans had surrounded them and too many were on top dancing about and beating out a rhythm, foreign and unpleasant. "There's a time and a place for that beat," he said to a *Melody Maker* reporter who had insinuated himself into the car. "But it isn't here!" Meanwhile, the instigator of this mob, Noel Whitcomb, fully sated, snuck off into a waiting taxi. He had a date at the race course, back in the normality of the press club with a pint of Guinness.

Somehow lost in the melee between the car and the train, Bill was soon minus his suede gloves, his overnight bag, and several buttons from his overcoat. Eventually he was rescued by policemen and carried aloft to the waiting train. But where was Cuppy? Still stuck in the car, now crying and holding a stuffed bear close to her heart. Coppers found her and conveyed her down a side track to a secluded part of the eight-coach Rock 'n' Roll Special, where she joined Bill and a local serenading group in a swaying compartment. Bill was perplexed, even a little angry. Why were they singing at him stuff he'd never recorded? Rival hits like "Hound Dog" and curious quasi-folk ditties like "Don't You Rock Me Daddy-O." Rory Blackwell, leader of the local group, tried to make himself heard above the din of chanting and the frequent massed cry of "HALEY!!" as the train passed a station. "You see, Mr. Haley," Blackwell shouted into his ear, "we can't afford a big band like yours with its electric and steel guitars. We love you, you're magic, but we have to scuffle up instruments to make our music. We call it skiffle. You must meet Lonnie Donegan, you'd like him."

At Waterloo there was more craziness, thousands of people disrupting rush hour. Bowlers and brollies were sent spinning. A fleet of Rolls-Royces conveyed Bill and his retinue by pushing a path through the mob, eventually reaching the posh Savoy Hotel in the heart of London. Cuppy cried all the way. Bill was thinking about a beverage. The *Daily Mirror* boys were rubbing their hands in glee. Next morning their front-page headline shouted FANTABULOUS!

Now to the proof of the pudding: the music, the act, the show. The tour, exclusively playing cinemas, started in London, went up north as far as Scotland and returned via Wales and even the Republic of Ireland. When the band played, the punters were well rewarded. The sound was as rattle-rocking as the records, from the opening "Razzle Dazzle" to the inevitable big finish of "Rock Around the Clock." Rudy Pompilli and Al Rex obliged with their vaudeville routine, straddling their instruments, lying on the stage, removing jackets to reveal suspenders. Franny Beecher sang a funny, high-pitched version of "You Made Me Love You." Bill presided over the proceedings like a ringmaster. Oh, it was a great show all right, but the audience had to wait a hell of a long time for it. And after paying premium prices, they felt short-changed at a mere thirty minutes.

In their old-fashioned wisdom the Grades, knowing nothing about rock 'n' roll, had preceded the star attraction with a bill tedious to big-beat fans and especially to Teds and Rockers. There was a comedy duo, a pennywhistler, and almost an hour of the Vic Lewis Orchestra, a well-oiled jazz organization that represented everything rock 'n' roll was against. The men in Dobell's shop would've been in heaven, but the Teds were outraged. "We want the Comets!" they chanted over the strains of slick flattened fifths.

With the Comets here and gone in a flash, there was a rebellion of slow clapping and "We want Bill!" No dice. Management played their ace, "God

Save the Queen," and the theater emptied because there was still a modicum of authority left in Britain. Afterwards, in the dressing room, Bill was up to his old trick of reassuring the press that he was no threat to the status quo. He apologized for the stage antics, explaining that this was only a way of making a living. Was the press aware that his guitarist used to be in the Benny Goodman Orchestra? That his drummer had done a stint with Glenn Miller?

Bill Haley finished his tour as a friendly sort of bloke but no god of the battle beat. Few, too few, were in Southampton to see him off when they left one dark March day. His chart reign was over. Snarling and pouting from across the ocean waited a band of real raucous rockers, and already their discs were spinning blue murder in the land of Shakespeare. Little Richard, Jerry Lee Lewis, Gene Vincent, and of course Elvis. All of them rocked because they needed to vent an inner anger, and, more tellingly, they reeked of eroticism. Haley remained the one-eyed cat, bewildered, longing to be home. "Glad it's all over," he wrote in his diary. "Just want to be tucked up at home. So tired."

Lots of money had been made on the British tour, but lots of pumping hearts and excited loins had been lost. Bill Haley and His Comets were not what they'd appeared to be. Said the London *Observer*: "Mr. Haley turns out to be a nice kid, just like us, who drinks milk and wants to make young people happy." That was a problem if you wanted rock longevity with an ending worthy of Valhalla. That Bill Haley was no longer hot was clear from the charts. Like a comet he had made spectacular dust and gas but now he was streaming off somewhere beyond the pop orbit. His records slipped away as the new boys moved up. "Rock Around the Clock," much revived, was to be Bill's signature tune, his only tune. Back at school I closed my file on Bill Haley, sorry to say. Elvis gripped me. Skiffle enabled me to buy a cheap guitar and flay and wail. No band, no scotch-plaid tux, no vaudeville. Do it yourself and on the cheap. The end of showbiz, the beginning of the British Invasion, and I was to roll in on that wave.

During the 1970s, when I'd started living in Hollywood, I found myself one night at a music venue called the Red Velvet. Dick Clark was there, and we said hello since Dick knew me from my days on his tours and singing on *American Bandstand* with my one big hit, "You Turn Me On." Being a gentleman and knowing of my interest in old-time rock 'n' roll, Dick introduced me to a chubby-faced fellow hovering behind him. "Say hello to Bill Haley." I certainly did, and later we retired to a corner where we chatted. Haley seemed kindly but watchful. He wasn't easy on the drinks, but then I'd always been fond of

Jack Daniel's, too. He treated me like a brother act and I remember him saying, "I guess, like you tell me, I was the first conductor on that rocking train. But I lost control somewhere along the way. We both just got caught up in it. We happened to be there at the time, the place, and the beat. We made our mark, didn't we? Didn't we?"

CHAPTER 14

WHEN THE CLOCK STRIKES TWELVE . . .

The year 1958 got off to a great start for the Comets but went downhill quickly. They toured in Canada and came back home to play on Dick Clark's *American Bandstand*. A single, "Skinny Minnie," cracked the Top 40—their first in over a year. They played for three weeks in Brazil and Argentina and were mobbed by fans. But the group's luck turned when they began a tour of twenty-three cities in Europe and two in North Africa. Their standing-room-only shows turned into the first full-out rock 'n' roll riots in Paris, Essen, and, especially, West Berlin, where they had to flee the stage of the massive Sports Palace as seven thousand fans trashed the place and caused tens of thousands of dollars' worth of damage. Since East Berlin teenagers were involved—the Wall had not yet been built—communist leaders and newspapers created a phony Cold War incident, denouncing the corrupting evils of this new American music and branding Haley a "rock 'n' roll gangster." Spanish authorities canceled their concerts and seized their equipment until the proper bribes were paid. All in all, because of extra police protection, stolen money, canceled shows, and other problems, the tour was such a financial disaster that Haley had to wire home for enough money to fly the band back to America.

That was only a warm-up for his troubles to come. Because of bad business deals, particularly the ones Lord Jim Ferguson made in Haley's name with Philadelphia mobsters, the Internal Revenue Service seized his real estate holdings and garnisheed his record and publishing royalties. He sidestepped them by signing a new contract with Warner Bros. Records in early 1960 to get his hands on a $50,000 advance before the company found out about his tax liens. Later that year, after his wife divorced him and won sizable child support and alimony judgments that effectively broke him, he fled to Mexico and became a fugitive for the next ten years, slipping back into the U.S. only now and then to pay off his mob debts by appearing in small Las Vegas clubs. The only time the Comets could play together was when a promoter set up an occasional date in South America, Europe, or India.

His original partners, Johnny Grande and Billy Williamson, called it quits. According to Grande, "By 1962 I realized that we had gone about as far as we were ever going to go in the business. The touring was becoming a grind. We ended up once in Mexico in a town so small there weren't any hotels. We ended up sleeping on canvas mats in an abortion clinic. It was time to come home and get on with my life." That left only Rudy Pompilli from the old days to hire "Comets" for periodic treks to odd spots around the world. By the time the Beatles arrived on U.S. soil in 1964, Bill Haley had already disappeared down America's memory hole.

But that didn't mean the end of his recording career. He enjoyed several Mexican hits on the Orfeon label, and started a new family with a young Latina wife in Vera Cruz. He was still sharing the stage with top acts during his overseas pilgrimages. In 1968 his summer tour through half a dozen European countries created such a sensation that radio stations began playing his old songs again. In Great Britain the original "Rock Around the Clock" returned to the charts. People wanted to dance again and groove to the sheer joy of the big-beat rhythm.

The following year, as Haley was negotiating with the IRS to settle his back taxes, New York talent agent Richard Nader booked him to headline the first Original Rock 'n' Roll Revival at Madison Square Garden's 4,500-seat Felt Forum, on October 18, 1969. Also on the bill were Chuck Berry, the Platters, the Coasters, the Shirelles, Jimmy Clanton, and a new vocal group called Sha Na Na. It was the greatest assemblage of fifties rock 'n' roll stars since Alan Freed's Brooklyn Paramount Theater shows ten years earlier. It was also one of 1969 America's most jarring anachronisms, because rock 'n' roll's early protagonists seemed so hopelessly lost in a time warp. Now was the Age of Aquarius, and it would have been impossible to imagine someone like Bill Haley, dressed in paisley bellbottoms, stepping out into the patchouli haze of Woodstock just a few months earlier and warning the assembled multitudes, "Don't take the

BILL HALEY *and* THE COMETS

Bill Haley moved to Mexico in 1960 to evade the IRS. He married a Vera Cruz girl, recorded for a Mexican company, and enjoyed several Latin American hits. He couldn't return legally to America until the late sixties.

pink dots," before tearing into "Rock Around the Clock." In fact, Sha Na Na had performed at Woodstock as a goof on rock 'n' roll, nudging and winking their way through songs like "Get a Job" to show 600,000-plus flower children that, yes, we're all so much hipper now and, really, how did anybody listen to this shit with a straight face?

But people who'd grown up in the fifties were beginning to miss it. Richard Nader recalled, "Everybody laughed at me. When I approached Madison Square Garden about doing a show there, the management tried to discourage me. They thought rock 'n' roll would make them look bad." But advance tickets sold so briskly that he had to schedule a second show, which also sold out. Bill Haley and His Comets brought down the house that night and got an eight-minute ovation. *The New York Times* called them "as exciting as almost anything heard lately." Two years later Nader moved his revivals into the Garden's twenty-thousand-seat Main Arena. "We sold out there, too. Through the seventies we put on twenty-five shows in the Main Arena, and twenty-one of them sold out. It was the longest-running concert series in Madison Square Garden's history."

By the early 1970s Americans were making references to a distinct cultural era called "the Fifties"—no longer the previous decade but a slab of fading history with its own symbols and memories, sealed off forever beyond the politically charged, chaotic sixties. Not since the years following "the Roaring Twenties" had a decade's numerical designation become shorthand for a way of life. In late 1971 a suburban New York folk singer named Don McLean tried to put some perspective between the fifties and seventies in a two-sided single called "American Pie" that spent four weeks at the top of the charts. (The *American Pie* LP was No. 1 for seven weeks.) The song, eight and a half minutes of cryptic lyrics that required footnotes, was pure late-sixties pretentiousness, but it was also McLean's admission that his generation had lost its direction after Buddy Holly's death on February 3, 1959—"the day the music died."

Two years later, youthful filmmaker George Lucas, remembering his own exhilaration at hearing "Rock Around the Clock" play over the opening credits of *Blackboard Jungle*, used the recording to similarly open *American Graffiti* as he introduced his cast of teenagers outside a drive-in diner, savoring their last bittersweet moments of carefree adolescence on graduation night, 1962. *American Graffiti* was a watershed film; its accompanying soundtrack LP of vintage hits went to No. 1 in late 1973 and stayed in the album charts for a year. When the film's star, Ron Howard, repeated his all-American preppie role in a wildly popular ABC-TV knockoff called *Happy Days*, Haley was called in to make a new recording of "Rock Around the Clock" as the show's opening theme song during its first two (1974–75) seasons. Decca reissued his original classic, and like a comet it came back around to visit the American Top 40 for the third time.

Though only eleven years separated *American Graffiti* from the spring weekend it depicted, the film was a period piece. Between 1962 and 1973, a U.S. president and two other major political leaders had been assassinated, a foreign war had divided the country, race riots had scarred a dozen major cities, the current president was on the verge of being thrown out of office, and kids were hung over from a hallucinatory binge. In short, 1973 America was in the grip of the same paranoia, weariness, and despair it had suffered after World War II and the Korean War. Folks needed a breather. The closest thing to American normality, or normalcy, seemed to be the 1950s. And *American Graffiti*, despite its 1962 time frame, was really about the American fifties, when cars were cooler, hair was higher, and screen monsters had buggier eyes.

In films from the fifties and sixties, whenever a teenager dropped a coin in the jukebox or flipped on the radio, out came generic music, usually a kind of big-band rock that aging movie producers considered hip (and cheap, since no licensing was required from record companies). Kids in the audience were left wondering, *Why don't they play some good records?* After *American Graffiti*, however, it seemed for a while that nearly every Hollywood film had fifties rock 'n' roll playing in the background.

The year 1973 also introduced the first fifties rock 'n' roll documentary, *Let the Good Times Roll*, filmed at Richard Nader's concerts at Nassau Coliseum on Long Island and at Detroit's Cobo Hall. The lineup, according to a *Rolling Stone* review at the time, "ranges from Chuck Berry, Little Richard and Fats Domino through the inconsequential reunion of Danny and the Juniors, the stale semi-burlesque act of the Shirelles, and the sophisticated and contemporary brashness of the Coasters (who are better seen in funky clubs than arenas—which is not to begrudge them the break of appearing in this movie)." The reviewer apparently forgot that Bill Haley and a Comets group was also on hand. The movie did not show these artists at their best—after all, they were fifteen years past their prime and trying to adjust not only to a seventies audience's expectations but also to a film medium that had developed in the late sixties around a more theatrical, social-oriented strain of rock music. But at least *Let the Good Times Roll* reminded a younger generation that rock music had a pedigree going back more than twenty years.

By 1978 rock 'n' roll biopics began showing up in theaters, including *American Hot Wax* (Alan Freed), *The Buddy Holly Story*, and *This Is Elvis*. But the most important film, and one of the year's top box-office smashes, was an adaptation of a stage play called *Grease*, whose soundtrack album stayed at No. 1 for twelve weeks and spawned four Top 10 singles. If any doubts remained about which cultural symbols represented 1950s America, *Grease* enshrined them in celluloid: high school hi-jinx, shark-finned cars, sci-fi flicks, bouffants, pastel shirts, first love, catchy rock 'n' roll tunes about all the aforementioned, and the spotlight dance.

The seventies gave rise to another phenomenon: the "oldies"-format radio station, dedicated to rock 'n' roll from roughly 1955 to 1965. (Oldies was short for "oldies but goodies," a 1940s radio term that Los Angeles disc jockey Art Laboe enshrined in 1959 with the first album of an *Oldies but Goodies* anthology series that survives to this day.) Up until the early 1990s, nearly two hundred of these stations thrived around the country, and many of them were leaders in their markets, including WCBS-FM in New York City. One 50,000-watt station in Hartford, Connecticut, covered six states, while another 50,000-watt powerhouse in Oklahoma City, calling itself a "retro formatics" station because its vintage deejays played old jingles to go along with the records, beamed out over most of the Southwest. In Los Angeles, KRTH-FM—known as K-Earth—was listed as one of the Top 15 "billing outlets" in the country, with an annual revenue so high that in 1993 a New York City corporation bought it for a then record $110 million.

Thanks to this fifties flashback, Bill Haley—with his spit curl now a comb-over plastered against a pasty, elongated forehead—was able to maintain a fairly busy schedule as a nostalgia act up through 1975, especially in the U.K. where "Rock Around the Clock" returned to the charts yet again (1974) and reached as high as No. 20. But the death of Rudy Pompilli brought the Comets crashing to earth. From then on Haley played with ragtag outfits whose members were often in conflict with each other. Lonely and out of touch, he often needed "minders" whose job was to make sure he showed up at gigs and recording sessions reasonably sober. His final European tours, in 1979, drew mostly scathing reviews capped with headlines like "Bill Haley—All That's Left Is the Curl." England's *Melody Maker* likened one of his performances to "watching your granddad embarrassing everyone by doing a rock 'n' roll routine at the local British Legion." His only triumph was a November command performance at London's Theatre Royal, where, after he sang an abbreviated "Rock Around the Clock," Queen Elizabeth greeted him with, "It was great to hear that music again. I grew up on it and it reminds me of when I was young."

Years of alcoholism and an inoperable brain tumor finally pushed him into a twilight of no return. Now bloated, broke, and living alone in the dusty Rio Grande Valley town of Harlingen, Texas, he wandered the streets like a disembodied soul, often hallucinating and shouting at people and being escorted home by sympathetic policemen. He developed a habit of making rambling, incoherent phone calls to old friends late into the night. Bill Haley died in his sleep, probably from a heart attack, on February 9, 1981, and was cremated three days later. He was fifty-five.

CHAPTER 15

ROCK TILL BROAD DAYLIGHT!

Bill Haley and His Comets' recording of "Rock Around the Clock" has passed through several corporations in the past four decades. In January 1962 a Hollywood talent agency, Music Corporation of America (MCA), bought Decca Records, changed its name to MCA Records, transported hundreds of boxes filled with tapes and transcription discs from New York to Universal City, California, and stored them behind the Manhattan subway facade on the backlot of Universal Studios. Nearly thirty years later, Matsushita Electric Industrial, a Japanese conglomerate, bought MCA Records and then unloaded it on Canada's Seagram Corporation when Japan's economy went sour. Seagram merged MCA with PolyGram Records and held onto them just long enough to sell everything, in 2000, to a French water and sewage management conglomerate named Vivendi, which subsumed the various record companies within an entity called Universal Music Group, now the world's largest record corporation. Through all this international churning and burning, the original Decca recordings of Bill Haley have remained in Universal City.

In early 2002 Los Angeles Superior Court Judge Victoria Gerard Chaney approved a $4.75-million settlement between Universal Music Group and at least three hundred recording artists who had been on Decca's roster before 1962. The lead plaintiff in the suit, singer Peggy Lee, accused Decca, MCA, and especially Universal of using "questionable accounting tactics" to cheat artists out of their royalties, beginning in the 1940s. Bill Haley and His Comets were included in the class action.

The song "Rock Around the Clock" has also passed through various hands. Traditionally publishers, who have the job of collecting royalties, own half a song and the songwriters own the other half. Up until 2001 the sole publisher was Myers Music, now a part of Sony/ATV Tunes in Nashville. Jimmy Myers and Max Freedman, as equal writers, split the remaining fifty percent. When Freedman died without children on October 8, 1962, his quarter interest in "Rock Around the Clock" went to his widow, Ray, who sold her rights sixteen years later to Max's former writing partner, Frank Capano, for $2,000. On December 28, 1980, Ray died, leaving her estate to her sister, Molly Goldstein.

According to the 1909 copyright law that covered "Rock Around the Clock," songwriters or their heirs could reclaim interest in a property when it came up for renewal twenty-eight years after the original copyright, so in 1981 Max Freedman's only living blood relative, his nephew Daniel Waldstein, renewed Freedman's 1953 copyright out from under Capano, then resold Capano the rights a year later for an undisclosed amount. Molly Goldstein, claiming inheritance of Freedman's renewal interest through his widow, sold the same piece of musical real estate to Jimmy Myers in 1983 for $10,000 and guaranteed royalties of at least $156,000. That immediately sparked a lawsuit by Capano (assignee of Waldstein) against Myers (assignee of Goldstein). When the court ruled in favor of Capano/Waldstein on February 5, 1985, Myers/Goldstein appealed, and the case was settled later that year with each side sharing undisclosed percentages of the Freedman copyright interest. Since 2001, the year of Jimmy Myers's death, the "(We're Gonna) Rock Around the Clock" copyright has been held jointly by Capano Music in Gibbstown, New Jersey, Myers Music c/o Sony/ATV in Nashville, and Robert Cinque of New York City.

With the advent of the compact disc in the early eighties, MCA recording engineers unfroze the past and brought "Rock Around the Clock" into the digital present—with all the attendant problems of switching from an old technology to a modern one. To create a new recording directly from the original compressed and equalized master tape would have impeded eighties playback with the restrictions of fifties engineering, and the digital process would have picked up those limitations and amplified them. So an engineer had to go back to the original studio master—Gabler's second-generation overdubbed tape—and recreate, with as much clarity and authenticity as possible, what the April 12, 1954, session sounded like on the other side of the microphones. The result closely resembles the familiar "Rock Around the Clock," yet something is different. We're hearing the tape instead of the record. You can hear the one-two count-off that set the downbeat for Billy Gussak's rim shots. A chair squeaks. Haley pops his *p*'s. The instruments don't have the same spatial relationship to each other as before. And the uncompressed bass is flooding the mix. This studio tape is fascinating to listen to, but is it the *real* "Rock Around the Clock"? You can't say it's been tampered with, because the tampered-with version is the one we've been listening to for the past fifty years. As a document, it's a more unadulterated version that sets history aright, like a never-seen "director's cut" of a film. But it's still not the same reproduction as the 1954 single of "Rock Around the Clock." It doesn't quite have the punch.

Andy McKaie, Universal Music's man in charge of catalog development, told writer Keri Leigh, "I think anyone who is in charge of reissue projects… has two responsibilities: 1) to music history, and 2) to the record company. They go hand in hand. You can't continue with this kind of specialty project if you're just putting out old music that isn't going to sell. You try to reach a happy compromise between what you know will sell and what's important to be archived in music history." McKaie said he's usually against making a record sound significantly different than it did originally. "I don't do it too much, because I feel you're messing with history. When you do that, you're changing people's memories. If you've got a good track and good masters, why monkey with it?" The only concession to the new technology, McKaie contends, should be that the recording sounds good "because now our ears are used to hearing such perfect sound quality…. [We] want it to sound the way it originally sounded, only cleaner."

In June 2002 Universal Music Group became one of the first major record companies to offer most of its catalog, including "Rock Around the Clock" and the rest of the Comets' recordings, for downloading over the Internet, beginning at ninety-nine cents a song. Today's listeners are more likely to hear "Rock Around the Clock" on their iPods than on a CD player.

Looking back at it now, "Rock Around the Clock" wasn't as revolutionary as the Comets' earlier hit, "Crazy Man, Crazy." It didn't have any slang to appeal to teenagers, and, if the sheet music or Sonny Dae's original rendition are any indication of its intrinsic qualities, it really wasn't all that great a song. But Bill Haley and His Comets transformed this plain piece of claptrap into a revelation. Writing in the *Wall Street Journal* in 2004, John McDonough observed, "Few pop recordings of the past century could be said to have had a more primal impact on the course of American music than 'Rock Around the Clock'…. And rock has been the life of the party ever since." British writer Michael

Satchell, in *U.S. News & World Report*'s tribute to American music in 2002, called the song "an exuberant, pulsating blend of guitars, sax, and piano, riding the beat of a slap-back bass and a whip-crack snare. It was utterly different from any music we had ever heard."

Of course, others are less impressed. Amy Taubin of the *Village Voice*, during a 1995 retrospective of *Blackboard Jungle*, blasted the film as a "contrived... wooden social-conscience flick [whose] fame rests on its being the first rock and roll movie," then called Haley's opening recording "just as stiff as anything that follows." British writer Chris Campling, discussing "Rock Around the Clock" in the *London Times* in 2004, dubbed it "a strange little pebble from which to build a monument. If ever there was an ugly duckling that became a humongous great multi-platinum swan, it's that one."

And what of Bill Haley? How does he stack up today? He has a star on the Hollywood Walk of Fame, on the southwest corner of Ivar Street and Hollywood Boulevard. He was inducted into the Rock and Roll Hall of Fame in Cleveland in 1987, the second year of voting. (Danny Cedrone's Gibson guitar has also been enshrined there.) That same year, he was portrayed by actor John Paramor in an Australian film called *Shout! The Johnny O'Keefe Story*, which covered the Comets' 1957 tour Down Under. And his face—along with Elvis Presley's, Buddy Holly's, and others'—graced a 29-cent U.S. postage stamp in 1993. Now, in 2005, actor Tom Hanks has announced that he's writing and will direct a biopic about Haley next year. But outside of "Rock Around the Clock," Bill Haley has mostly been forgotten, a comet rather than a star.

Jazz guitarist Skip Heller said, "Once [Haley] found out what a Bill Haley record sounded like, that's what a Bill Haley record sounded like." He would not—and perhaps could not—change. As writer Colin Escott put it, "Repetition set in. No one needed the new Bill Haley record because they had the old one." Worse, Haley insisted on recording mostly songs he owned, which meant he was singing "Rockin' Rollin' Schnitzlebank" and "Whoa Mabel!" when he should have been getting first crack at "Lonesome Town" or "Great Balls of Fire."

Ultimately, though Haley was a more professional musician with a superior, precision band, he couldn't compete with the Elvis Presley brigade of rockabillies. "Young audiences demanded real emotion," wrote John McDonough, "and the more raw and unpolished the music sounded, the more authentic it seemed." Despite his importance to musical history, Bill Haley turned out to be the Rodney Dangerfield of rock 'n' roll, bereft of respect.

On June 16, 1993, along with Buddy Holly, Eddie Cochran, and a couple of other fifties rockers, Bill Haley—without the Comets—was honored by the U.S. Postal Service with a 29-cent stamp.

Though Haley has been gone now for almost twenty-five years, the Comets are still very much alive as a rock 'n' roll troupe. In late 1987—the year Haley, without the group, was inducted into the Rock and Roll Hall of Fame—the Philadelphia Music Foundation contacted Bill Turner, who had played guitar with the Comets in the early seventies, and asked him to invite the original members to play at its gala First Annual Philadelphia Music Awards Show at the prestigious Philadelphia Academy of Music. Turner passed the word to retired schoolteacher and part-time actor Dick Richards, who in turn hunted down his old mates Franny Beecher (a superintendent at a local Halloween costume factory), Joey D'Ambrosio (a Las Vegas pit boss), Johnny Grande and Marshall Lytle (both retired from music and operating their own businesses in Florida), and Billy Williamson. All agreed to show up for the awards show except Williamson, who had turned his back on his music career to the point of never even discussing it. On the night of the awards, what was left of the 1954–55 Comets walked onstage together for the first time in thirty-two years. They performed "Rock Around the Clock" with Lytle singing lead. Beecher played Cedrone's famous solo, but, as always, he was unable to duplicate the fluid slide leading back into the verse.

Buoyed by the reception they got, the old-timers decided to regroup. They found a young English vocalist named Jacko Buddin who sounded roughly like Haley and took their act to Europe, where an enthusiastic fan base was waiting for them. Since they were enjoined from calling themselves the Comets because the group's later bassist, Al Rappa, owned the name, they trademarked their group the Original Comets. In 1997, when the author saw them at the House of Blues in West Hollywood, they impressively recreated the big-room, big-beat bop of their classic recordings in front of a packed house. Two years later they recorded a CD for rockabilly producer Ronny Weiser's Rollin' Rock label that was as close to the Pythian Temple sessions as they were likely to get. At this writing, in early 2005, these stalwarts, now in their seventies and eighties, are still touring around the world. This past March, during a trip to Hollywood for a 50th anniversary screening of *Blackboard Jungle*, they met Glenn Ford, the film's star, for the first time.

The clock has run out on most of the principals in the "Rock Around the Clock" story: Danny Cedrone (1954), Fred F. Sears (1957), Max C. Freedman (1962), Alan Freed (1965), Sam Katzman (1973), Louis Jordan (1975), Rudy Pompilli (1976), Jack Howard (1976), Bill Haley (1981), Sam Theard (1982), Hal Hogan (1985), Dave Miller (1986), Paschal Vennitti/Sonny Dae (1987), Richard Brooks (1992), Billy Gussak (1995), Billy Williamson (1996), Milt Gabler (2001), Jimmy Myers (2001), Alan Dale (2002), and Bill Randle (2004) are deceased.

But "Rock Around the Clock" rocks on.

CHAPTER 16

FOR THE RECORD

Bill Haley's recordings have made a successful transition to digital, but anyone looking to run out and buy a Bill Haley CD should be warned up front that you want his 1950s Decca material, which has been reissued either by MCA, Universal Music, or Geffen Records. His later recordings are hit and miss, but mostly miss. Haley recut "Rock Around the Clock" for at least half a dozen companies, most notably in 1960 for Warner Bros., and these recordings should probably be avoided by the casual fan. There is only one "Rock Around the Clock," and if the sleeve or the back card doesn't make clear that the track inside is the 1954 hit version, it probably isn't.

The best current CD of Bill Haley's Decca recordings, including his biggest hits—from "Shake, Rattle, and Roll" to "See You Later, Alligator"—is *Rock Around the Clock* (Geffen Records B0001705-02), a 2004 package that commemorates the fiftieth anniversary of "Rock Around the Clock." This CD duplicates the front and back cover art of the 1955 Decca LP and contains its twelve songs, plus three bonus tracks—all in their original mono (see www.UniversalChronicles.com).

For the Bill Haley fanatic who wants everything, leave it to German thoroughness. Bear Family Records' *Bill Haley & His Comets: The Decca Years and More* (BCD 15506) is a five-CD box set from 1990 that contains their 1954–59 Decca output, including alternate takes of some of the later stereo recordings, as well as two demos—106 tracks in all. The box also contains a large colorful booklet with over 150 photos and illustrations (www.bear-family.de).

The raw but exciting recordings by the Saddlemen and the early Comets on the Holiday and Essex labels are available on *The Best of Bill Haley and His Comets 1951-1954* (Varese Sarabande 302 066 549 2). "Crazy Man, Crazy," "Rocket 88," "Rock the Joint," "Real Rock Drive," and fourteen other tracks trace Bill Haley's journey from jive cowboy to rockin' cat (www.varesesarabande.com). An earlier British CD of this material with a couple of additional tracks, on Roller Coaster Records, can be found at www.rollercoasterrecords.com.

The Comets' April 17, 1955, Cleveland concert is available on *Bill Haley & His Comets Rock 'N' Roll Show* (Hydra BCK 27105). The group performs "Rock Around the Clock" twice on this German CD, with Haley and Billy Williamson providing the guitar solos. Also included are live versions of "Crazy Man, Crazy," "Rock the Joint," "Shake, Rattle, and Roll," "Dim, Dim the Lights," and ten other songs. The tape is mono and not of pristine studio fidelity. The booklet has some rare photos (www.rockithydra.de).

Also available on Hydra Records is *Bill Haley and His Comets Onscreen* (BCK 27107), a 1997 CD of nineteen live tracks from 1954 to 1958. Included are performances of "Rock Around the Clock" on the Ed Sullivan and Ray Bolger TV shows in 1955 and at a 1956 Alan Freed concert at the Brooklyn Theater—all featuring Franny Beecher playing the guitar solos. The CD also includes the Comets' three songs in the 1954 Universal-International film short, *Round Up of Rhythm*, and their live version of "Rudy's Rock" recorded at Columbia Studios for the film *Rock Around the Clock*. As one might expect from recordings taken from various sources, the sound quality varies.

A third Hydra CD, from 2001, is *Bill Haley & His Comets on the Air* (BCK 27112), with two full live shows, including interviews, recorded at the Armed Forces Network Studio in Frankfurt, Germany, in 1962. These are among the last recordings of the Comets before Johnny Grande and Billy Williamson departed. Johnny Kay plays lead guitar on "Rock Around the Clock" and the other tracks. Sound quality is generally good.

For obsessives, Hydra has recently (2004) released a two-CD set called *Bill Haley & Friends, Volume 3—50 Years of Rock Around the Clock* (BCK 27128-1.5), containing sixty different recordings of "Rock Around the Clock," half of them by

Bill Haley and His Comets (including a couple of unreleased tracks) and the rest by artists from all over the world. Here's your chance to hear the original Sonny Dae and His Knights version.

Two dozen recordings by the Jodimars, the group composed of three defecting Comets, can be found on *Let's All Rock Together* (Rockstar RSRCD 007). This 1994 British CD also includes two Bill Haley interviews from 1957 and 1968 (www.bim-bam.com).

And finally, the Original Comets' 1999 album, *Still Rockin' Around the Clock* (Rollin' Rock CD 103), shows the early members—Joey D'Ambrosio, Marshall Lytle, Johnny Grande, Dick Richards, and Franny Beecher—revisiting their old hits, including, naturally, "Rock Around the Clock."

Anyone looking for a list of every known recorded performance of "Rock Around the Clock" by Bill Haley should check with the Rockabilly Hall of Fame at www.rockabillyhall.com.

For those who collect shellac or vinyl, there's plenty of stuff to find in used record shops or on eBay. Discs are fairly inexpensive except for Haley's rare, early hillbilly 78s. Between 1954 and 1956, the single "Rock Around the Clock"/"Thirteen Women" by Bill Haley and His Comets was released all over the world on both 45 and 78. Here is an incomplete list. Most foreign releases were on 78 rpm.

Decca 29124 (78) (Old logo; Personality Series) 1954
Decca 29124 (78) (Old logo, pink promo; Personality Series) 1954
Decca 29124 (45) (Old logo) 1954
Decca 29124 (78) (New logo) 1955
Decca 29124 (45) (New logo) 1955
Decca 29124 (45) (New logo, pink promo) 1955
Decca 05317 (red label) (UK, 78) 1954
Brunswick 05317 (UK, 78) 1955
Brunswick 05317 (UK, 45) 1955
Decca 50 005 (France) 1954
Brunswick 86044 (France) 1955
CID US 90504 (France, *Blackboard Jungle* tie-in) 1956

Decca FM 6290 (South Africa) 1956
Decca 50001 (Uruguay, red label) 1956
Decca 333422 (Argentina) 1956
Decca 288612 (Brazil) 1956
Coral PD 9151 (South Africa, 45) 1956
Rhythm 5317 (Finland, 78) 1956
Festival FS 841 (78) (Australia & New Zealand) 1956
Festival SP45-679 (45) (Australia & New Zealand) 1956
Fonit 1999 (78) (Italian) 1956

Haley's "Rock Around the Clock" was also issued with other B-sides.
Essex 102 (bootleg) w/ "Crazy Man, Crazy" 1955
Brunswick 12031 (Germany) w/ "A.B.C. Boogie" 1956
Decca G-21017 (Canada) w/ "Shake, Rattle, and Roll" 1956
Decca DE-329 (Japan) w/ "Shake, Rattle, and Roll 1956
Columbia 24090 (Spain) w/ "Birth…Boogie"/"Mambo Rock" 1956

The following Bill Haley LPs were released in 1954–56. The first album was called *Shake, Rattle, and Roll*. All others were titled *Rock Around the Clock*, except where noted.
Decca DL 5560 (10-inch) (Jalopy cover) 1954
Decca DL-8225 (12-inch) (red "ROCK" cover) 1955
Brunswick LAT 8117 (UK) (red "ROCK" cover) 1955
Brunswick 86043 (Germany, 12-inch) (red "ROCK" cover) 1955
Brunswick 86044 (Germany, 10-inch) (green cover, Comets photo) 1955
Brunswick 86043 (French) 1955
Festival FR 12-1102 (Australia) 1956
Decca 78225 (Canada) 1956
Decca SLP-7001 (Brazil, 10-inch) (photos from *RATC* movie on cover) 1956
Columbia CGE 60148 (Spain) 1956
CID US 223596 (French 10-inch) *Rock Around the Clock du film "Graine de Violence"* 1956

The following Bill Haley EPs were released in 1954–56. Decca 2168 was called *Shake, Rattle, and Roll* and had the same jalopy cover art as the *Shake, Rattle, and Roll* LP. The others were called *Rock Around the Clock*.
Decca 2168 1954

Brunswick 9250 (UK)(red label) ("ROCK" cover, same as US & UK 12-inch LP) 1955
Decca 9250 (UK) (red label) (same cover as above) 1955
Festival DX-10840 (Australia) (grandfather clock cover) 1956
Brunswick 10027 (French) (group photo) 1956
CID 105512 (French) *Rock Around the Clock du film "Graine de Violence"* 1956
Columbia CGE 60148 (Spain) 1956
Coliseum 990 (Thailand) 1956
Decca EP 55 (Japan) (jitterbugging couple cover) 1956

Earlier songs called "Rock Around the Clock":
Mercury 8196 (78 only) Hal Singer 1950
Dot 1099 (78 only) Wally Mercer 1952

Earlier version of *the* "Rock Around the Clock":
Arcade 123 Sonny Dae and His Knights 1953

This is an incomplete list of cover records of "Rock Around the Clock" in 1955–56. Some of them were issued on budget discs with two popular songs on each side rendered (often badly) by studio musicians.

MGM 12028 Charles Wolcott/The MGM Studio Orchestra
Tops R258-49 (budget) Fred Gibson/The Bill Allen Orchestra
Gilmar RX114 (budget) Fred Gibson/The Bill Allen Orchestra
Bell 1098 (budget) The Four Bells/Jimmy Carroll Orchestra
Broadway 301 (budget) Jack Richards/Vic Corwin Orchestra
Gateway 1124 (budget) Dick Warren
Prom 1118 (budget) Gale Drake/Prom Orchestra (7-inch 78)
HMV HR 62 (New Zealand) Johnny Cooper
HMV 113 (UK) The Deep River Boys
Electrola 8573 (Germany) The Deep River Boys
Dixie 882/3 The Dixie Harmonaires
Embassy WB 161 (U.K.) The Canadians
Columbia 631/20437 (Argentina) Frontera & Band
MarVela 1259 (Puerto Rico) Los Hispanos
King CL-182 (Japan) Eri Chiemi
Q.R.S. Word Roll 9164J Lawrence Cook (piano roll)

ACKNOWLEDGMENTS

Thanks to Mary Katherine Aldin, Dick Blackburn, Trevor Cajaio, Ray Campi, Anthony Capano of Capano Music, Jim Carlton, Stuart Colman, Lee Cotten, Joey D'Ambrosio, Bob Doerschuk, Art Fein, Peter and Lynda Ford, Alex Frazer-Harrison, Ed Friedland, Chris Gardner, Galen Gart, Libby Goold, Denise Gregoire, John Haley, Skip Heller, David Hirschberg, Rik Hull, Mary Jane Isles, Richard Johnston, the late Herbert Kamitz, Klaus Kettner, Kenny Kirby, Allen Larman, Eric LeBlanc, the late Bill Leibowitz, Marshall Lytle, Ronnie Mack, Hugh McCallum, Big Jay McNeely, the late Jimmy Myers, Richard Nader, Bill Nolan, Jim Philbrook, Steve Propes, Eric Prudoehl, Ray Regalado, Earl Reinhalter, Jeff Riley, Glenn Robison, Deb H. Smith, Gloria Stanford, Dickie Thompson, Bob Timmers of the Rockabilly Hall of Fame, Steve Valdez, Dan Vanore, John von Hoelle, Rockin' Ronny Weiser, Ian Whitcomb, Jonny Whiteside, Morgan Wright, the Long Beach Public Library, the Los Angeles Public Library, and the Academy of Motion Picture Arts and Sciences for graciously helping me put this book together.

BIBLIOGRAPHY

Articles

Ackerman, Paul. "R&B Tunes' Boom Relegates Pop Field to Cover Activity." *Billboard*, March 26, 1955, p. 18.

Ackerman, Paul. "Country & Western Music Fans Like Their Talent Alive." *Billboard*, May 21, 1955, p. 1.

Ackerman, Paul. "Death Certificate Premature; R&B Ain't Ever Been Sick." *Billboard*, July 23, 1955, p. 18.

Armstrong, Roger. "Tape Research, Part 2." *Ace Records Newsletter: Right Track*, September 2000, p. 6.

Arneel, Gene. "America's 107 Million-$ Films." *Variety*, January 25, 1956, p. 1.

Blackburn, Bob. "Inventor of Rock 'N Roll Defends His Type of Music for Teenagers." *Ottawa Citizen*, July 17, 1956, p. 17.

Bundy, June. "DJ Surveys Show Top Jocks May Not Be Best Pluggers." *Billboard*, February 5, 1955, p. 14.

Campling, Chris. "Clock That Rocked the World." *London Times*, April 9, 2004, T2, p. 12.

Cotten, Lee. "The Original Comets: 240 Years of Rock 'n' Roll." *Rock & Blues News*, October–November 1999, p. 5.

Cotten, Lee. "The Jodimar Years." *Rock & Blues News*, December '00–January '01, p. 21.

Colman, Stuart. "Call Me Shorty." *Now Dig This*, June 2001 (# 219), p. 6.

Cromelin, Richard. "J. Myers; Co-Wrote 'Rock Around the Clock.'" *Los Angeles Times*, May 12, 2001, p. B9.

Crowther, Bosley. "Blackboard Jungle." *New York Times*, March 27, 1955, p. 21.

Escott, Colin. "Bill Haley: Indisputably—The First." *Goldmine*, April 19, 1991, p. 12.

Finnis, Rob. "Don't Knock the Rock." *New Kommotion*, #24, 1966, p. 26.

Ford, Peter. "'Rock Around the Clock' and Me." *Now Dig This*, June 2004 (#255), p. 15.

Friedman, Joel. "Disk, Film Industries Find Bliss in Union." *Billboard*, February 5, 1955, p. 1.

Gardner, Chris. "Welcome Home, Bill!" *Now Dig This*, April 2004 (#253), p. 20.

Gellner, Arrol. "WWII Gave Rise to Drywall Interiors." *Los Angeles Times*, December 14, 2003, p. K9.

Grande, John. "Rocking Around With Bill Haley." *Radio-TV Mirror*, February 1957, p. 28.

Green, Jesse. "The Song Is Ended." *New York Times Magazine*, June 2, 1996, p. 28.

Haley, Bill. "Diaries: January–March 1956." *Now Dig This*, January 1996 (#154), p. 8.

Haley, Bill. "Diaries: April–July 1956." *Now Dig This*, February 1996 (# 155), p. 24.

Haley, Bill. "Diaries: January–March 1957." *Now Dig This*, January 1997 (#166), p. 17.

Healy, John, Chuck Philips, and P.J. Huffstetter. "Latest Spin on Online Music." *Los Angeles Times*, June 13, 2002, p. C1.

Hirschberg, David. "Calling All Comets: The Reunion of Bill Haley's Comets, Vol.1." *Now Dig This*, June 1988 (#63), p. 18.

Hirschberg, David. "Calling All Comets: The Reunion of Bill Haley's Comets, Vol.2." *Now Dig This*, July 1988 (#64), p. 24.

Hirschberg, David. "Belated News of the Death of Billy Williamson." *Now Dig This*, June 1997 (#171), p. 2.

Hirschberg, David. "Franny Beecher: The Beak Speaks." *Now Dig This*, June 1997 (#171), p. 15.

Holden, Stephen. "Hardened Youths in a Staider Era." *New York Times*, August 25, 1995, p. C12.

Hollinger, Hy. "Controversial Pic Backfires." *Variety*, September 14, 1955, p. 5.

Horowitz, Is. "45 Disks Gain Edge Over 78 Pop Singles." *Billboard*, February 26, 1955, p. 27.

Johnson, Jon. "The Original Comets Soar Again." *Country Standard Time*, April/May 2000, p. 38.

Johnson, Reed. "*Playboy* at 50: A Man's Notes." *Los Angeles Times*, November 28, 2003, p. E1.

Leigh, Spencer. "Freddie Bell, 1995." *Now Dig This*, May 1995 (#146), p. 17.

Leisner, Pat. "Hit Makers of the '50s Keep on Ticking." *Los Angeles Times*, June 22, 2001, p. F19.

Manna, Sal. "*Blackboard Jungle* Revisited," *Los Angeles Herald-Examiner*, January 13, 1983, p. B1.

Martin, Joe. "Music-Record Year Ends Up With Bang." *Billboard*, January 8, 1955, p. 1.

McDonough, John. "Bill Haley's Truly Golden Oldie." *Wall Street Journal*, April 8, 2004, p. D8.

Mehren, Elizabeth, "Decades of Devotion Squeezed Into Three Days," *Los Angeles Times*, July 20, 2004, p. A13.

Moonoogian, George. "Baby, That's Rock 'n' Roll." *Bop Magazine*, #1 (self-published), 1982, p. 1.

Myers, Gary. "Bobby Charles—See You Later, Alligator." *Discoveries*, May 1993, p. 26.

Obrecht, Jas. "Q/A: Milt Gabler." *Guitar Player*, August 1981, p. 16.

O'Neill, Ann W., and Jeff Leeds. "Judge Clears Proposed Settlement in Royalty Suit Against Universal." *Los Angeles Times*, January 16, 2002, p. C1.

Pekar, Harvey. "The Development of Modern Bass." *Down Beat*, October 11, 1962, p. 15.

Rolontz, Bob. "Lush Days Over; Oldtimers Give Young Pop Artists Rough Time." *Billboard*, May 29, 1954, p. 9.

Satchell, Michael. "Birth of the Cool." *U.S. News & World Report*, July 8–15, 2002, p. 57.

Schoenfeld, Herm. "Artists, Angles and A&R Headaches With Singers Plugging Own Tunes." *Variety*, June 8, 1955, p. 1.

Schonberg, Edith. "You Can't Fool Public, Says Haley." *Down Beat*, May 30, 1956, p. 10.

Taubin, Amy. "Man on the Verge." *Village Voice*, August 29, 1995, p. 54.

Thurber, Jon. "Milton Gabler; Promoted Jazz, Rock." *Los Angeles Times*, July 29, 2001, p. B14.

Woodford, Chris. "Wow! Those Riotous Rock 'n' Rollers." *Now Dig This*, April 1994 (#133), p. 21.

Wozniak, Mary. "Bonita Man Co-Wrote Smash." *News-Press* (Lee County, FL), October 21, 2000, p. 1A.

"Alan Freed Attracts Mob in Newark." *Billboard*, May 15, 1954, p. 14.

"ASCAP Publisher Roster Zooms Over 750; Writer Members Total 3,200." *Variety*, November 2, 1955, p. 51.

"'Blackboard' Court-OK'd for Atlanta; City Ducks Basic Censorship Issue." *Variety*, July 13, 1955, p. 7.

"'Blackboard Jungle' $8,000,000 Gross." *Hollywood Reporter*, May 31, 1957, p. 3.

"'Blackboard Jungle' Acquired By MGM." *Hollywood Reporter*, April 13, 1954, p. 1.

"'Blackboard Jungle' Shapes as Top Metro Release in Some Time." *Variety*, May 1, 1956, p. 5.

"Controversy Adds Fuel to 'Blackboard Jungle' Big Bonfire Abroad." *Variety*, December 2, 1955, p. 1.

"Crazy Man Haley." *Hit Parader*, October 1953, p. 14.

"Decca Brass Hit L.A. for Meetings." *Billboard*, January 29, 1955, p. 18.

"Decca Credits 'Jungle' With Re-Winding 'Clock.'" *Variety*, June 22, 1955, p. 49.

"Decca Finishes '54 With 20% Increase." *Billboard*, January 8, 1955, p. 13.

"Decca Tops Best-Seller C&W Charts, as Majors Keep Hold." *Billboard*, April 9, 1955, p. 18.

"Decca Uses All Media in Promotion Step-Ups." *Billboard*, March 12, 1955, p. 20.

"Deejay Freed Opens B'klyn Para to Flesh." *Billboard*, February 1955, p. 25.

"'53 Disk Sales Hit All-Time Peak of $205,000,000." *Billboard*, May 8, 1954, p. 13.

"'55 Platter Sales Up 40% Over '54." *Variety*, December 28, 1955, p. 1.

"First Big Rock 'n' Roller, Bill Haley, Dies." *Baton Rouge State-Times*, February 10, 1981, p. 9A.

"$4,000,000 U.S. B.O." *Daily Variety*, September 31, 1955, p. 9.

"Freed Ball Takes 24G at St. Nick." *Billboard*, January 22, 1955, p. 13.

"Haley's 'Clock' Disk Nears 2,000,000 Mark." *Variety*, November 30, 1955, p. 1.

"Haley's Disks Hit 3 Million." *Billboard*, July 2, 1955, p. 16.

"'Jungle' Gets Tie-Ins by Everybody." *Billboard*, February 19, 1955, p. 25.

"Majors and Subsids Switch to 45's for Pops to Deejays." *Billboard*, June 5, 1954, p. 14.

"Many Exhibs Fear Col's Rock 'N' Roll 'Clock' May Time-Fuse Teenage Antics." *Variety*, April 11, 1956, p. 1.

"Martin Block Blasts Current Pops." *Variety*, July 6, 1955, p. 41.

"Memphis Mayor Rescinds Censor's 'Jungle' Ban, Okays Pic for 'Adults.'" *Variety*, April 13, 1955, p. 1.

"Metro Cuts 'Blackboard' Footage to Enable Film Pass Milwaukee Muster." *Variety*, May 20, 1955, p. 1.

"Metro Fights Atlanta Lady Censor Who Banned 'Blackboard Jungle' Outright." *Variety*, June 8, 1955, p. 5.

"Milwaukee Threatens to Shutter Theater Unless 'Blackboard Jungle' Cuts Are Made." *Variety*, May 19, 1955, p. 8.

"Mixed Global Reaction to 'Blackboard'." *Variety*, November 30, 1955, p. 16.

"Phono Makers' Output in '53 Registers Whopping Increase." *Billboard*, May 15, 1954, p. 34.

"Phono Men See RCA Cut Cueing Demise of 78s." *Billboard*, January 8, 1955, p. 11.

"Police Seek to Finger 'Blackboard Jungle' as Root of Hooliganism." *Variety*, May 18, 1955, p. 5.

"Rackmil Pegs Rise on Diversification." *Billboard*, March 19, 1955, p. 15.

"Release of 'Jungle,' 'Bamboo' Irks Jap Censors." *Variety*, September 21, 1955, p. 14.

"'Rock Around the Clock' Raises Rumpus in Britain; Many Towns Ban Pic." *Variety*, September 19, 1956, p. 2.

"State Dept. Upholds Luce's 'Blackboard' Blast in Answer to Arthur Loew's Complaint." *Daily Variety*, September 22, 1955, p. 1.

"Victor Readies New Push in R&B Field." *Billboard*, February 12, 1955, p. 19.

Books

Boorstin, Daniel. *The Image: Or What Happened to the American Dream*. New York: Atheneum Books, 1961.

Crist, Judith. *Take 22: Moviemakers on Moviemaking*. New York: Viking Penguin, Inc., 1984.

Colcord, Joanna C. *Songs of American Sailormen*. New York: Norton, 1938.

Collins, Tony. *Rock Mr. Blues: The Life & Music of Wynonie Harris*. Milford, NH: Big Nickel Publications, 1995.

Cotten, Lee. *Did Elvis Sing in Your Hometown?* Sacramento, CA: High Sierra Books, 1995.

Cotten, Lee. *Shake, Rattle & Roll: The Golden Age of American Rock 'N' Roll, Vol. 1*. Ann Arbor, MI: Pierian Press, 1989.

Dawson, Jim, and Steve Propes. *What Was the First Rock 'N' Roll Record?* Winchester, MA: Faber & Faber, 1992.

Dawson, Jim. *Nervous Man Nervous: Big Jay McNeely & the Rise of the Honking Tenor Sax*. Milford, NH: Big Nickel Publications, 1994.

Dawson, Jim, and Steve Propes. *45 RPM: The History, Heroes & Villains of a Pop Music Revolution*. San Francisco: Backbeat Books, 2003.

Ehrenstein, David, and Bill Reed. *Rock on Film*. New York: Delilah Books, 1982.

Foster, Pops, as told to Tom Stoddard. *The Autobiography of Pops Foster: New Orleans Jazzman*. San Francisco, CA: Backbeat Books, 2005.

Haley, John W., and John von Hoelle. *Sound and Glory: The Incredible Story of Bill Haley*. Wilmington, DE: Dyne-American Publications, 1990.

Harrison. Daphne Duval, *Black Pearls: Blues Queens of the 1920s*. New Brunswick, NJ: Rutgers University Press, 1988.

Hunter, Evan. *The Blackboard Jungle*. New York: Simon & Schuster, 1954/1999.

Jasen, David. *Encyclopedia of Tin Pan Alley*. New York: Routledge, 2003.

Jones, LeRoi. *Blues People*. New York: Morrow Quill Paperbacks, 1963.

Kantor, Bernard L. et al., *Directors at Work*. New York: Funk & Wagnalls, 1970.

Marshall, J.D. *Blueprint for Babylon*. Los Angeles: Phoenix House, 1978.

McGee, Mark Thomas. *The Rock and Roll Movie Encyclopedia of the 1950s*. Jefferson, NC: McFarland & Company, Inc., 1990.

Miller, James. *Flowers in the Dustbin*. New York: Simon & Schuster, 1999.

Ottley, Leroi, and William A. Weatherby. *The Negro in New York: An Informal Social History*, New York: Oceana Publications, 1967.

Porterfield, Nolan. *Jimmie Rodgers: The Life and Times of America's Blue Yodeler*. Urbana, IL: University of Illinois Press, 1979.

Shapiro, Helen. *Walking Back to Happiness*. London: HarperCollins, 1993.

Shaw, Arnold. *The Rockin' '50s*. New York: Da Capo Press, 1974.

Shaw, Arnold. *Honkers and Shouters*. New York: Collier Books, 1978.

Terkel, Studs. *Talking to Myself*. New York: Pantheon Books, 1977.

Wertham, Fredric. *Seduction of the Innocent*. New York: Rinehart & Co., 1954.

Waters, Ethel. *His Eye Is on the Sparrow*. Garden City, NY: Doubleday & Co., 1951.

Whitcomb, Ian. *After the Ball: Pop Music From Rag to Rock*. New York: Simon & Schuster, 1972.

Websites

www.billhaley.co.uk
www.billhaley.de
http:/freespace.virgin.net/wjc.haley/discography/main.html
www.hoyhoy.com
www.rhull.freeserve.co.uk
www.rockabillyhall.com
www.rockabilly.net
www.history-of-rock.com/haley.htm

Recordings/Liner Notes/Other

Dae, Sonny & His Knights, *Rockaphilly*, Rollercoaster ROLL 2001, 1980s.

Haley, Bill & His Comets, *The Decca Years* (notes by Colin Escott), Bear Family BCD 15506, 1990.

Haley, Bill & His Comets, *Bill Haley & His Comets: Rock 'n' Roll Show* (notes by Klaus Kettner), Hydra BCK 27105, 1997.

Haley, Bill & His Comets, *On Screen* (notes by Klaus Kettner & Tony Wilkinson), Hydra BCK 27107, 1998.

Haley, Bill & His Comets, *Rock the Joint!—The Original Essex Recordings 1951–1954* (notes by Chris Gardner), Rollercoaster SKR 1529, 1994.

Jodimars, *Let's All Rock Together* (notes by David Hirschberg), Rockstar RSRCD 007, 1994.

Theard, Sam, *In Chronological Order 1929-1936*, Document DOCD-5479, 1996.

Rock Around the Clock film booklet, Columbia Pictures, 1956.

Recorded Interviews with Bill Haley

Lister, Monty, Liverpool, England, February 20, 1957.

Lister, Monty, Warrington, England, May 3, 1968.

Pewter, Jim, New York City, October 18, 1969.

Robinson, Red, Vancouver, Canada, spring 1966.

Scott, Roger, London, England, 1977.

ABOUT THE AUTHOR

Jim Dawson is the author of half a dozen books on early popular music, including *What Was the First Rock 'n' Roll Record?*—which Mojo called "one of the most impressive musical reads of the year"—and *45 RPM: The History, Heroes & Villains of a Pop Music Revolution* (Backbeat Books). He also wrote the 1999 comedy bestseller *Who Cut the Cheese? A Cultural History of the Fart*. Dawson divides his time between Hollywood, California, and his native West Virginia.

PHOTO CREDITS

Pages 58, 61, 73 & 81: courtesy of Klaus Kettner/Hydra Records.

Page 66: courtesy of Deb H. Smith and Mary Jane Isles.

Page 76: courtesy of Dickie Thompson.

Page 84: courtesy of Janet Cedrone Alvarez.

Page 116: courtesy of The Glenn Ford Library & Archives.

Page 117: courtesy of Homer Van Pelt/The Glenn Ford Library & Archives.

INDEX

A
Allsman, James "Slim," 31, 34
American Bandstand, 168, 170
American Graffiti, 173–74
"American Pie," 173
Anderson, Leroy, 64
ASCAP (American Society of Composers, Arrangers and Producers), 137–38
Autry, Gene, 27, 28, 58

B
Ballen, Ivin, 62–63
Barbour, J. Berni, 14, 16
Barnard, Julian "Bashful Barney," 32
Bass, history of, 37–38
Beecher, Francis "Franny," 135–36, 140, 167, 181
Berman, Pandro, 115, 116–17
Bernard, Al, 93, 94
Berry, Chuck, 9, 171
Bill Haley and His Comets
   "Crazy Man, Crazy" recorded by, 50–54
   Decca Records signs, 68–70
   formation of, 48–49
   internal conflicts within, 140–41
   lineup of, 48, 65, 68, 92, 141
   at the Masonic Temple (Cleveland), 127–28
   in movies, 143–54
   at the Original Rock 'n' Roll Revival, 171–73
   popularity of, 5–6, 135–36, 140
   recordings of, 183–84
   "Rock Around the Clock" recorded by, 6, 8, 10, 64, 80–87, 90–92, 96, 128–30, 133
   "R.O.C.K." recorded by, 149, 151–52
   "See You Later, Alligator" recorded by, 147, 151
   "Shake, Rattle, and Roll" recorded by, 93–96
   on television, 135, 170, 184
   "Thirteen Women" recorded by, 73–80, 87–92
   on world tour, 156–57, 163, 165–68, 170
Blackboard Jungle, 86, 113–26, 128, 129, 159, 180, 182
Black Swan Records, 13–15, 26
Blackwell, Rory, 167
Blues, 11–17
BMI (Broadcast Music, Inc.), 137–38
Boccelli, Richard, 54
The Boswell Sisters, 17, 18
Bradford, Perry, 12–13
Brooks, Richard, 113–18, 121, 126, 182
Brunswick Records, 21
Buck, Clarence, 16
Buddin, Jacko, 181
Buono, Art, 65, 66, 82–83

203

C

Capano, Frank, 178
Cash, Johnny, 10
Cedrone, Danny, 45–47, 51, 63, 78–80, 83–86, 93, 96, 135, 180, 182
Charles, Ray, 10
Checker, Chubby, 154–55
Cinque, Robert, 178
Clare, Sidney, 17
Clark, Dick, 5, 168, 170
Cochran, Eddie, 10
Constantine, Al, 32
Cook, Shorty, 28, 30
Cooke, Sam, 10
Country music, 27–32
Cowboy Records, 60
"Crazy Blues," 13, 51
"Crazy Man, Crazy," 50–54

D

Dale, Alan, 154, 182
D'Ambrosio, Joey, 65–66, 68, 73, 78, 80, 83, 84, 86, 92, 128, 140–41, 153, 181
Davis, Sammy, Jr., 85
A Day in the Life of a Famous DJ, 143
Dean, James, 54–56
Decca Records, 21, 61, 68–73, 87–88, 92–93, 128, 133, 173, 177
Diddley, Bo, 9–10
DiMucci, Dion, 10
Domino, Fats, 10, 95
Don't Knock the Rock!, 153–54
The Down Homers, 28, 30, 32

E

Essex Records, 53, 68

Everly, Don and Phil, 10

F

Ferguson, James "Lord Jim," 39–40, 46, 72, 81, 94, 140–41, 166, 170
Ferko String Band, 42, 58
Fitzgerald, Ella, 17
Ford, Glenn, 117, 118, 126, 182
Ford, Peter, 117
Ford, Tennessee Ernie, 47, 51
45s, 87–88, 89, 133
Foster, George "Pops," 37
4 Aces of Western Swing, 31–33
Fox Trot, 88–89
Francis, David "Panama," 93
Freddie Bell and His Bellboys, 149, 153, 165
Freed, Alan, 5, 9, 127, 132–33, 141, 147, 148, 174, 182
Freedman, Max C., 12, 24, 42, 57–64, 178, 182

G

Gabler, Milt, 68–75, 77–81, 85, 87, 88, 92, 93, 151, 182
Glory in the Flower, 54, 56
Golden West Cowboys, 31, 35
Goldstein, Molly, 178
"Good Rockin' Tonight," 19, 24, 43
Grade, Lew and Leslie, 165, 167
Grande, Johnny, 34–41, 44, 48, 73, 78, 79, 84, 86, 92, 140, 141, 171, 181
Grease, 175
Great Britain, rock 'n' roll in, 157–69
Guitar solos, 83
Gussak, Billy, 47–48, 50–51, 54, 71, 80, 82, 85, 86, 93, 182

H

Hager, Fred, 12–13
Haley, Bill. *See also* Bill Haley and His Comets
   as ambassador of rock 'n' roll, 155
   birth and childhood of, 26–28
   death of, 176, 182
   early music career of, 28–33
   Elvis Presley meets, 141–42
   later years of, 155–56, 170–72, 175–76
   legacy of, 180–81
   recordings of, 182–87
   and the Saddlemen, 35–48
Handy, William C., 11, 13
"Harlem Blues," 12–13
Harris, Wynonie, 18–19, 24, 43
Hawkins, Erskine, 17
Higler, Charlie, 48
Hogan, Hal, 65, 66, 81, 182
Holly, Buddy, 10, 173
Honking, 65–68
Hope, Lynn, 67
"Hound Dog," 149
Howard, Jack, 31–32, 60, 65, 182
Howard, Ron, 173

J

Jacquet, Illinois, 67
Jem Publishing, 60
The Jodimars, 141, 184
Jones, Ralph, 141, 153
Jordan, Louis, 21, 22–23, 68, 69, 74, 182
Joyce, Jolly, 143, 144, 149, 165, 166
Juvenile delinquency, 118–20, 126, 131–32

K

Kapp, Jack, 68

Katzman, Sam, 144–45, 149, 151, 153, 154, 182
Kekuku, Joseph, 35–36
King, Pee Wee, 31, 35
King, Tex, 32
Kings of Rhythm, 40

L

Lee, Peggy, 177
Lennon, John, 5, 6
"Let the Good Times Roll," 22–24, 69
Let the Good Times Roll (documentary), 174
Lewis, Jerry Lee, 10
Liquori, Anthony, 65
Little Richard, 10, 153
Lucas, George, 173
Luce, Clare Boothe, 121
Lymon, Frankie, 10
Lytle, Marshall, 43–46, 48, 50, 71, 78, 83, 84, 86, 92, 127, 129, 140–41, 153, 181

M

Mambo, 128
Martinez, Tony, 149
Massaro, Salvatore, 45
McIntire, Larry, 71–72, 85, 86
McKaie, Andy, 179
McLean, Don, 173
McNeely, Big Jay, 67–68
Melody Manor, 163, 165
Mercer, Wally, 25
MGM, 113–16, 121
Miller, Al, 42
Miller, Dave, 40–42, 46, 48, 50, 53, 64, 70, 182
Miller, Emmett, 27, 28
Miller, Paul, 42

"My Daddy Rocks Me," 16, 22
Myers, Jimmy, 33, 38, 39, 58–62, 64–65, 68, 71–72, 85–86, 116, 178, 182
Myers Music, 33, 60, 62, 178
"My Man Rocks Me (With One Steady Roll)," 14–15, 19, 27, 64

N

Nader, Richard, 171, 173, 174
Nelson, Ricky, 10
"New Rubbing on That Darned Old Thing," 21–22

O

The Original Comets, 182, 185
The Original Dixieland "Jass" Band, 11–12, 89
Original Rock 'n' Roll Revival, 171–73

P

Pace, Harry H., 13
Palda Records, 42
Peer, Ralph, 27
Perkins, Carl, 10
The Pied Piper of Cleveland, 141–43
The Platters, 149, 165, 171
Pollar, Lou, 31
Pompilli, Rudy, 141, 153, 167, 171, 175, 182
Presley, Elvis, 5, 10, 56, 69, 127, 141–42, 145, 149, 155, 156, 157
Preston, Jimmy, 27, 31, 43

R

Randle, Bill, 127, 141–43, 182
The Range Drifters, 30
Rappa, Al, 182
"Real Rock Drive," 47, 48–49

Rebel Without a Cause, 54, 55
Rex, Al, 38, 41, 43, 141, 153, 167
Rhythm and blues, 8, 18–19, 21–24, 31, 130–31
Richards, Dick, 80, 81, 92, 94, 127–28, 135, 140–41, 153, 181
"R.O.C.K.," 149, 151–52
"Rock and Roll," 17, 18, 19
"Rock Around the Clock"
 as beginning of rock 'n' roll, 5, 6, 9–10
 Bill Haley and His Comets' original recording of, 6, 8, 10, 64, 80–87, 90–92, 96
 impact of, 179–80
 Max C. Freedman writes, 24, 61–64
 ownership of, 177–78
 popularity of, 6, 91–92, 133–34
 recordings of, 183–87
 reissues of, 128–30, 133, 173, 178–79
 sales of, 5, 133, 140
 Sam Theard's, 24–25
 Sonny Dae & His Knights', 24, 65, 80, 81–82
 in soundtrack of *American Graffiti*, 173
 in soundtrack of *Blackboard Jungle*, 115–18, 124–25, 128
 on television, 135
 Wally Mercer's, 25
Rock Around the Clock (movie), 145–53, 162–63
"Rocket 88," 40–41, 43, 46
"Rockin' Rollers Jubilee," 17
"Rock It for Me," 17
Rock 'n' roll
 beginning of, 5, 6, 9–10, 132–33
 criticisms of, 137–40, 152–53, 155

206 ROCK AROUND THE CLOCK

growth of, 133
meanings of, 17, 18
movies featuring, 144–55, 173–75
on oldies-format radio stations, 175
origins of term, 14, 15
"Rock the Joint," 39, 43, 45–46, 62, 83
Rodgers, Jimmie, 27–28, 36, 89
"Round the Clock," 19
Ryerson, Art, 50–51, 80, 135

S
The Saddlemen, 35–48, 184
Sears, Fred F., 145, 151, 154, 182
"See You Later, Alligator," 147, 151
"Shake, Rattle, and Roll," 93–96
Shake, Rattle and Rock, 95
Shamblin, Eldon, 45
Sha Na Na, 171–72
Singer, Hal, 24
"Sioux City Sue," 58
Slaughter, Marion Try, 27
Smith, Mamie, 12–13, 51
Smith, Trixie, 13–14, 16, 26–27, 64
Sonny Dae & His Knights, 24, 65, 66, 80, 81–82
"Spo-Dee-O-Dee," 21
Steel guitar, history of, 35–36
Stone, Jesse, 93
Swing, 17–18
"The Syncopated Clock," 64

T
Taylor, Billy, 139–40

Teds, 161–63
Theard, Sam, 20–25, 69, 182
Thiele, Bob, 138
"Thirteen Women," 73–80, 87–92
Thomas, Dick, 57–58
Thompson, Dickie, 74–77
The Treniers, 51, 52–53, 153–54
Turner, Big Joe, 93, 94, 95, 140, 165
Turner, Bill, 181
Turner, Ike, 40

U
Universal Music Group, 177, 179

V
Vennitti, Paschal, 65, 182
Vincent, Gene, 10

W
Waldstein, Daniel, 178
Waters, Ethel, 26
Wertham, Fredric, 131–32
Whitcomb, Noel, 165, 166
Whiting, Richard, 17
The Wild One, 123
Williams, Hank, 43, 82
Williams, J. Mayo, 20, 21
Williamson, Billy, 34–37, 41, 44, 47, 48, 78, 79, 84, 92, 127–28, 135, 140, 171, 181, 182
WPWA, 31–32, 36, 39, 41, 48
Wyler, William, 113

Y
"You Rascal, You," 21

WHEN IT COMES TO MUSIC, WE WROTE THE BOOK.

All Music Guide to Rock
Third Edition
By Richie Unterberger
"Best rock guide of the year."
—*The Seattle Times*
Get the ultimate guide to the artists and recordings that really rock. Reflecting the ever-evolving world of rock, pop, and soul, this book reviews 12,000 albums by 2,000 performers—everything from rockabilly to British Invasion, Motown, folk rock, psychedelic rock, funk, punk, R&B, hip-hop, and more.
Softcover, 1,399 pages, 29 charts, ISBN 0-87930-653-X, $29.95

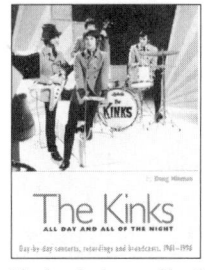

The Kinks
All Day and All of the Night
By Doug Hinman
With the help of band members, author Doug Himan has reconstructed the Kinks' meteoric rise to fame in the early '60s through their final breakdown in the '90s. The book also profiles Ray Davies, one of the most gifted songwriters in popular music. The book's day-by-day format details their entire concert history, all known recording sessions, and much more.
Softcover, 352 pages, ISBN 0-87930-765-X, $24.95

Studio Stories
How the Great New York Records Were Made: from Sinatra to the Ramones
By David Simons
Some of the best moments in New York's recording history, as seen by the producers, engineers, songwriters, and artists who made them happen. This book explores the ingredients that made the era unique—artists performing live in vibrant recording spaces; engineers spontaneously creating new effects and techniques; and, most important, recording studios that had life, character, and a signature sound.
Softcover, 224 pages, ISBN 0-87930-817-6, $24.95

Unknown Legends of Rock 'n' Roll
Psychedelic Unknowns, Mad Geniuses, Punk Pioneers, Lo-Fi Mavericks & More
By Richie Unterberger
In the background and the underground of rock 'n' roll since the '50s, hundreds of musicians have made great music but never made it to the top. Discover why some of history's brightest stars fizzled out, and hear the sounds they created along the way. This book with CD celebrates dozens of unknowns like the Great Society, Nick Drake, and the Monks.
Softcover w/CD, 422 pages, ISBN 0-87930-534-7, $19.95

The Hits Just Keep on Coming
The History of Top 40 Radio
By Ben Fong-Torres
Here's the whole crazy tale of the most powerful radio format of all time. It's got the stories behind the DJs, the fans, the singles, the jingles, commercials, dedications, contests, and requests—all "the platter chatter that matters." Reads like Top 40 radio itself: fast and fun.
Softcover, 272 pages, ISBN 0-87930-664-5, $19.95

Turn! Turn! Turn!
The '60s Folk-Rock Revolution
By Richie Unterberger
Read the acclaimed history of folk-rock's early years. Drawing on over 100 first-hand interviews with such artists as Roger McGuinn, Donovan, Judy Collins, John Sebastian, and Arlo Guthrie, the narrative weaves the stories of all the important innovators: Bob Dylan, the Byrds, Lovin' Spoonful, Buffalo Springfield, and dozens more.
Softcover, 320 pages, ISBN 0-87930-703-X, $19.95

AVAILABLE AT FINE BOOK AND MUSIC STORES EVERYWHERE, OR CONTACT:

Backbeat Books
6600 Silacci Way • Gilroy, CA 95020 USA
Phone: Toll Free (866) 222-5232 • Fax: (408) 848-5784
E-mail: backbeat@rushorder.com • Web: www.backbeatbooks.com